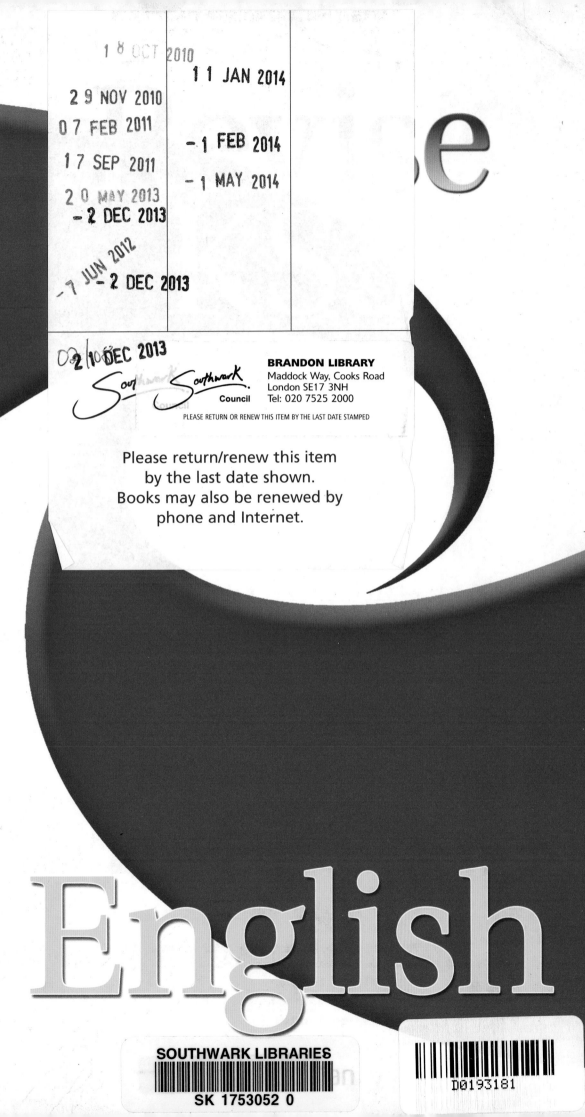

Please return/renew this item
by the last date shown.
Books may also be renewed by
phone and Internet.

English

Contents

English at Key Stage 3

Introduction to English at KS3

This book is designed for you to use at home to support your study at school. The topics covered in each chapter meet the requirements of the **National Curriculum for English** at Key Stage 3.

The National Curriculum separates English into three Attainment Targets.

Attainment Target 1 – Speaking and Listening

Throughout Key Stage 3 you will learn and develop skills that will enable you to communicate more effectively. You will learn to speak confidently and fluently in a range of formal and informal situations. You will also explore a range of roles in group work including: contributing, supporting and managing discussion. You will improve your listening skills and your ability to interpret tone of voice and gestures.

Attainment Target 2 – Reading

During your three years of study you will have the opportunity to read and respond to a range of texts: **plays, novels, poetry, non-fiction** and **media**. You will read modern **texts and writing from other historical periods**, including plays by **Shakespeare**. The skills you will develop are: **reading for research, reading for meaning,** and **understanding the author's craft**. You will have the opportunity to practise different reading techniques for different purposes.

Attainment Target 3 – Writing

Through your reading you will identify a range of techniques used to create particular effects in writing. You will learn to manage these techniques to make your own writing more effective. The major writing styles you will develop are: writing to **imagine, explore, entertain**; writing to **inform, explain, describe**; writing to **analyse** and **comment**; and writing to **persuade** or **argue**. You will also learn to **plan, draft** and **present** your work to make the most of the skills you have learned.

The National Literacy Strategy

The **National Literacy Strategy Framework for English at Key Stage 3** identifies each of the key skills and requirements of the National Curriculum. You will find information about National Literacy Strategy objectives in the margin throughout most chapters of this book.

The Framework for English is organised into **word, sentence** and **text level**.

Word and Sentence level

In each chapter you will find **Word level** and/or **Sentence level** panels. These panels will give you advice about: **specific spelling rules, vocabulary choices, sentence grammar** and **Standard English**. This information is usually related to the main content of the page or pages you have been studying and is intended to support your text level study.

Text Level

You will notice that the reading and writing chapters in this book often use the same texts. This will help you to identify particular techniques and then try them out in your own writing.

How this book will help

National Curriculum Levels

There is information about how to achieve each **National Curriculum Level (4–7)** at the beginning of each **chapter.** This information will help you to identify the skills you need to improve and develop. Most students aim to achieve **Level 5 or 6** by the end of **Year 9.**

Speaking, Listening, Reading and Writing

The book is separated into four main sections. The first three cover the Attainment Targets: **Speaking and Listening, Reading** and **Writing.** Each section will help you to learn, develop and revise the important skills in each area.

The Reading and Writing chapters aim to provide range, development and extension to cover Years 7 to 9. The **Shakespeare** topic in **Chapter 2** is particularly aimed at Year 9 and preparation for SATs.

The final section covers **spelling, punctuation** and **grammar.** Here you will find strategies to improve your **spelling** and a helpful reference guide to enable you to refine your **punctuation** and make conscious decisions about the **grammatical structures** you use.

Questions

Each chapter has a range of questions and tasks that will help you to test your level of understanding and refine your skills, as well as preparing you for **Optional Tests** in Years 7 and 8 and **SATs** in Year 9.

This book will help you to **check your progress and understanding** in four ways:

Progress Check tests

Have a go tasks

Optional Test questions

SATs questions.

Checking your progress

Progress Checks

At the end of each **topic** in the **Speaking and Listening, Reading** and **Writing** sections you will find a short **Progress check** test that covers the key points in that topic. Each question usually requires a true or false, multiple choice or one-word answer. The answers are printed upside down at the bottom of the test panel. Use these tests immediately after completing a topic to ensure that you understand the main points.

Have a go tests

In the **Speaking and Listening** and **Writing** sections you will find slightly longer **Have a go** tasks which extend the examples given in the topic you have studied. This is your chance to practise the new skills you have learned.

Optional Tests (Years 7 and 8)

Your school may have decided to use the new **Optional Tests** for **Years 7 and 8**, in which case you will find the questions at the end of each chapter useful for your revision. **However**, some schools do not use these exams; if your school is not using the Optional Tests you will probably have some kind of 'end-of-year test' and you may find the practice questions useful. Some answers and general guidance can be found at the back of the book on pages 148–152.

Remember: in English you are constantly developing and extending key reading and writing skills. End-of-year tests in Year 7 and Year 8 are an important part of your preparation for SATs in Year 9.

SATs questions (Year 9)

At the end of each chapter in the **Reading** and **Writing** sections you will find questions designed to help you revise for the **Key Stage 3 SATs in Year 9**. These examples will give you the chance to practise all the question styles you might expect in the final SATs exams. General guidance for answering these questions can be found at the back of the book on pages 148–152.

Preparing for SATs

In English your revision should focus on practising skills rather than learning facts. Follow these steps for successful revision.

STEP 1

Identify the skills that you have weaknesses in.
Ask your class teacher to help you with this where necessary.
Prioritise your revision topics and make a revision timetable or diary.

STEP 2

Study the topic to be learned.
Work through the examples.
Annotate the texts you are working on and make notes.
Learn key terms and techniques.

STEP 3

Attempt practice questions.
Focus on the skills identified in the topic you have studied.
Make sure you allow the correct amount of time for each question.

STEP 4

Compare your answers to the examples in the topic you have studied.
Identify areas of weakness that need further development.

STEP 5

Review your notes, annotations and exam answers for each
topic regularly.

GOOD LUCK!

1 Speaking and listening

After studying this section you should be able to:

● talk and listen with confidence in conversations
● join in group discussions
● understand how drama can help with your English studies

To achieve the following National Curriculum levels you need to

Level 4

● talk and listen with confidence in a range of situations
● ask questions and respond to the ideas of others

Level 5

● talk and listen with confidence in formal situations
● engage the interest of the listener by varying tone, pace and vocabulary

Level 6

● take an active role in discussion, showing awareness of the views of others
● make fluent use of Standard English

Level 7

● organise talk to communicate ideas clearly
● make significant contributions to discussion and manage the contributions of others
● use Standard English with confidence and fluency

1.1 Speaking and listening

Speaking and listening is not tested in any formal examinations at Key Stage 3. However, it is a very important element of your studies in Years 7, 8 and 9. Your English teacher will decide on the levels you receive for speaking and listening and this assessment will form part of your final Teacher Assessment level at the end of Year 9.

Some of the activities you take part in will be quite formal and assessed in an obvious way; however, at other times your teacher will be making informal judgements about your speaking and listening work without you even realising it. For this reason, it is important that you make the most of all of your speaking and listening opportunities.

Tasks you might expect

You might expect to carry out the following tasks:
● asking questions in class
● answering questions in class
● giving a talk (formal or informal)
● reading aloud.

Asking questions

This is an excellent way to **improve your levels of understanding**. Asking a question does not always mean that you don't understand what your teacher is talking about. Even if you do understand everything, you should still ask questions. It allows you to look beneath the surface for less obvious meanings. You will be given credit for asking intelligent and searching questions.

Answering questions

You should always attempt to answer questions in group discussions or oral tests. Even if you get the answer wrong, **you will be given credit for thinking and trying your best**. If you don't feel sure of an answer you should still have a go. You may have approached the problem from another angle or thought of something that your teacher did not consider. It does happen!

Reading aloud

This is a skill that can only be developed with practice. Always speak clearly and stand or sit up straight. **Read according to the punctuation to maintain the sense of what you are reading**. Think about the content of the piece you are reading and try to express the emotions of the characters you are reading by varying the pace and tone of your voice.

Giving a persuasive talk

In **Chapter 8** you will learn about writing a **persuasive speech** or talk. However, writing the speech is only half the skill – the way you present it is just as important.

The speech printed on page 10 is an extract from one of the most powerful and influential speeches of the twentieth century. It is the final part of a speech delivered by the Reverend Martin Luther King at a civil rights march in Washington DC, in the United States, on the 28th August 1963.

Key Point In order for a speech to be effective, in addition to being well written it must be delivered in a persuasive and powerful way.

As you read the speech, think about how you would deliver it. How would you give emphasis to the important parts of the speech?

Some of the key words and phrases have been highlighted for you.

So I say to **you, my** friends, that even though **we** must face the difficulties of today and tomorrow, I still **have a dream**. It is a **dream** deeply rooted in the American dream that one day this nation **will rise up** and live out the true meaning of its creed – **we** hold these truths to be self-evident, that all men are created equal.

* * * *

I have a dream that my four little children will one day live in a nation where they will not be judged by the colour of their skin but by the content of their character. **I have a dream today!**

* * * *

This is **our hope**. This is the **faith** that I go back to the South with.

With this **faith** we will be able to bear out of the mountain of despair a **stone of hope**. With this **faith** we will be able to transform the jangling discord of our nation into a beautiful symphony of brotherhood.

With this **faith we will be able to** work together, to pray together, to struggle together, to go to jail together, to stand up for freedom together; knowing that **we will be free one day**. This will be the day when all of God's children will be able to sing with new meaning – 'my country 'tis of thee; sweet land of liberty, land where my fathers died, land of the pilgrim's pride; from every mountain side, let **freedom** ring' – and if America is to be a great nation, this must become true.

So let freedom ring from the prodigious hilltops of New Hampshire.

Let freedom ring from the mighty mountains of New York.

Let **freedom** ring from the heightening Alleghenies of Pennsylvania.

Let **freedom** ring from the snow-capped Rockies of Colorado.

Let **freedom** ring from the curvaceous slopes of California.

But not only that.

Let **freedom** ring from Stone Mountain of Georgia.

Let **freedom** ring from Lookout Mountain of Tennessee.

Let **freedom** ring from every hill and molehill of Mississippi, from every mountain side, let **freedom** ring.

You should be able to:
- identify the main methods used by presenters to explain, persuade, amuse or argue a case.

How to give emphasis to your speech

- **Vary the pace** – the first part of this speech is written in long, complex sentences. This style lends itself to the speaker speeding up slightly towards the climax of the sentence. The final part of the speech is written in one-sentence paragraphs. This allows you to slow the speech down and emphasise each point.
- **Think about the rhythm** – the repetition in this speech, particularly within the sentences, helps to create a powerful rhythm.
- **Tone of voice** – think about how to deliver each section of the speech.

Will you sound hopeful, sad, angry or joyful? Will you speak at the same volume throughout the speech? Once you have the attention of the audience, you could lower the volume slightly to make people listen more carefully.

- **Emphasis** – think about particular words and phrases that may require more emphasis.
- **Gestures** – think about ways in which you could give more emphasis to your words through your hand gestures and facial expressions. Remember, open gestures, such as showing your palms, suggest honesty; clenched fists suggest power; and closed gestures such as folded arms suggest defence or dishonesty.

Progress Check

Have a go

1 Read this speech out loud, experimenting with the way you give emphasis to different parts of the speech.

2 If you write your own speech after working through the tasks in Chapter 8, practise delivering it in a persuasive way. Ask friends or family to be your audience.

1.2 Group discussion

Tasks you might expect

You might expect to carry out the following tasks:
- **informal paired discussion**
- **informal group discussion**
- **formal debate.**

Informal discussion

You will often be asked to discuss work in small groups (not just in English). The subject might be a poem, a character's strengths and weaknesses, a new approach to a problem or a social issue. The key to success is to **speak and listen**. This will allow you to share information and develop new ideas before presenting them to a larger group. You will lose marks if you remain silent and just listen. You will also lose marks if you are aggressive or you talk too much and ignore the ideas of others.

Key Point

If you are not confident in speaking and listening, then try to note down at least one point or question and make sure you use it in the debate or discussion.

Formal debate

There are rules and procedures to follow in a debate, which your teacher will explain to you. The important thing to remember is that you must use

Standard English. Do not use slang, colloquialism or dialect words. A debate is about listening to others as well as putting your own point across. You will develop a much stronger argument if you listen and respond to the points made by the opposition. **Make sure that you listen to their points and respond to them, as well as putting forward your arguments.**

> **Key Point**
>
> If you are confident about speaking in a group, then help others by asking supportive questions to bring in a weaker member of your group or by reinforcing a point made by somebody else.

Roles in group discussions

You will be given the opportunity to take on a **range of roles** when you take part in group work. Read through the guidelines below and try to apply them in your group work at school.

> **Key Point**
>
> In group work you will be asked to lead, contribute or support. In a formal debate the roles are more clearly defined: chairperson, proposer and seconder, opposer and seconder.

You should be able to:
- adopt a range of roles in discussion, including acting as spokesperson, and contribute in different ways.

Leading

If you are leading the group you will need to:
- **organise** the group
- **plan** how to complete the task
- keep other students **on task**
- **summarise** the main points made by others
- **identify differences** of opinion and help to **resolve** them
- **change the direction** of the discussion or refocus the task.

Contributing

If you are a contributor to the discussion, you will need to:
- **introduce** new ideas
- **express your opinion** and **respond** to the opinions of others
- **share** ideas and information
- **listen attentively.**

Supporting

If you are asked to support others, you will still have the opportunity to contribute as above, but you should also:

- **ask others specific questions**, in order to bring them into the discussion
- **encourage others** to continue
- **build on the ideas of others**, reinforcing their points.

Sentence level

There are many differences between speaking and writing. The key points that typify speech are:

- we rely on **tone, pace, facial expression and gestures** to get meaning across – in writing we have to rely on punctuation to do this
- speech is usually **spontaneous**, whereas writing is often planned
- we don't always speak in full sentences and speech can be interrupted
- vocabulary is often more **informal**, especially in conversation
- we use **non-standard forms** when talking informally
- sentence structure is much looser because speech often includes 'fillers': *you know, sort of, like* and hesitations: *er. . ., um. . . .*

1.3 Drama

At your school you may study drama as part of your English lessons, or you may have separate drama lessons as part of your timetable. However drama is organised at your school, you will probably find that your English teacher uses some drama techniques with you as part of your English studies. You may even use drama techniques such as **hot seating** and **improvised role-play** in other school subjects.

Why is drama important?

Not everybody enjoys acting and performing, but even if you don't want to be an actor in the future, drama is very important.

Drama helps you to develop many important life skills:

- **working as a team**
- **communicating clearly**
- **problem solving**
- **developing trust**.

Drama can also help you with your studies in English. It helps you to:

- **empathise** with characters
- **explore** the inner thoughts, feelings and motivations of characters in fiction
- **understand** the techniques used by Shakespeare and other playwrights you might study.

Drama techniques you might use

> **Key Point**
>
> The term **in character** means that you should speak, behave and react as the character you are playing, **not** as yourself.
> A **stimulus** is a piece of information, such as a picture, a prop or a few lines of dialogue to use as a starting point for a piece of drama.

Hot seating

With this technique one person sits in the 'hot seat', **in character**. The rest of the group, who are not in character, take it in turns to ask the character in the hot seat questions about their decisions, motivation, thoughts about what has happened in the scene and so on. The person in the hot seat must answer in character.

This technique can be very helpful in **exploring the inner thoughts and feelings of a character** in a novel or play you are studying in English lessons.

Thought tracking

This is another useful technique for exploring the inner thoughts and feelings of a character.

You may be given the command to **freeze** during work on a **scripted** or **improvised** scene. If you are spotlighted or tapped on the shoulder, you should speak out loud the thoughts and feelings of your character at that point in the scene.

Tableaux

A **tableau** is a still picture or image, also known as a **freeze frame**. It could be a key moment in a scene, frozen in time. This is useful because it gives the audience more time to take in what is happening. You can use **tableaux** to illustrate emotions, ideas and relationships. This technique is also useful for creating definite beginnings and endings for pieces of drama.

> **Word level**
>
> Many words in the English language are borrowed from other languages: **tableau** is French. Tableau forms its plural by adding an **x**. Other French words commonly used in English follow the same rule:
> tableau → tableaux, gateau → gateaux, bureau → bureaux.

Improvisation

When you **improvise** you make up a scene **without** working from a script. Improvisation can be **spontaneous** or **rehearsed**. Spontaneous improvisation is made up on the spot in response to a given **stimulus**. The scene is performed without rehearsal or preparation. In rehearsed improvisation, you are given time to prepare and practise, making alterations and improvements as you go.

Script work

When you work with a script you should respond to the **stage directions**. Think carefully about the character you are playing and what you want to do with the basic information you have about that person. Think about the way you want your character to **move and speak**, and **what they look like**. Try to find one or two **props** that help you to identify with the character you are playing.

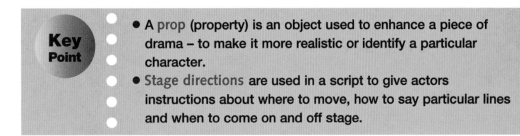

Key Point

- A prop (property) is an object used to enhance a piece of drama – to make it more realistic or identify a particular character.
- Stage directions are used in a script to give actors instructions about where to move, how to say particular lines and when to come on and off stage.

Progress Check

Have a go

1 Make sure you get the chance to practise each of the group talk roles in your class work.

2 Plan a talk on a subject you are interested in. Make a tape recording of your talk so you can work out how to improve your performance.

3 Choose a passage from your reading book and practise reading aloud at home.

4 Discuss the news, your homework or recent events in your favourite soap opera with a friend or your family.

2 Reading fiction and plays

After studying this section you should be able to:

- understand characters and their development
- comment on the setting of stories and plays
- understand relationships and their development
- understand the importance of openings
- study the plays of Shakespeare in an informed way

To achieve the following National Curriculum levels you need to

Level 4

- recognise what the characters are like
- have a general understanding of the whole text
- show an understanding of the plot

Level 5

- begin to read beneath the surface for meaning
- note the effect of particular words and phrases
- show some understanding of the feelings and behaviour of the characters

Level 6

- support your ideas about characters and relationships with detailed reference to the text

- write in some detail about the writer's use of language and the structure of the text
- comment on the creation of setting and atmosphere
- give a personal response to the text

Level 7

- show understanding of the more complex feelings of the characters
- recognise what the writer is trying to achieve and how they do this
- trace the development of plot, character and relationships and themes
- give a personal and critical response to the text

2.1 Characters

Character descriptions

In order to write convincing descriptions, an author needs to know the characters very well. Authors don't necessarily describe the character in detail – they may drop in clues about personality as the story progresses. J K Rowling, the author of the *Harry Potter* stories, claims to have a complete history for all of her characters in her head.

Appearance

The way a character looks gives the reader important clues about what kind of person they might be. Descriptions are vital in helping the reader to imagine what the character looks like. Vivid descriptions make characters seem real, even if they are a little unusual! Read the following description of Albus Dumbledore, from *Harry Potter and the Philosopher's Stone*.

> Nothing like this man had ever been seen in Privet Drive. He was tall, thin and very old, judging by the silver of his hair and beard, which were both long enough to tuck into his belt. He was wearing long robes, a purple cloak which swept the ground and high-heeled, buckled boots. His blue eyes were light, bright and sparkling behind half-moon spectacles and his nose was very long and crooked, as though it had been broken at least twice. This man's name was Albus Dumbledore.

First impressions

The above extract is the first description of the wizard, Albus Dumbledore, in the book. From this description the reader makes some initial judgements about the character – he is:
- unusual
- mysterious
- magical
- wise.

Dumbledore is the first wizard character to be introduced in the book, and in this description the fact that he is very different from the inhabitants of Privet Drive is emphasised. His **magical qualities** are also highlighted by the use of words like *silver*, *bright* and *sparkling*.

False impressions

Some descriptions can be **misleading**. Sometimes writers try to create a particular impression of a character so that they can surprise the reader later.

Read the following descriptions of Rubeus Hagrid. What is your first impression of the character?

> If the motorbike was huge, it was nothing to the man sitting astride it. He was almost twice as tall as a normal man and at least five times as wide. He looked simply too big to be allowed, and so *wild* – long tangles of bushy black hair and beard hid most of his face, he had hands the size of dustbin lids and his feet in their leather boots were like baby dolphins. In his vast, muscular arms he was holding a bundle of blankets.
>
> * * * *
>
> A giant of a man was standing in the doorway. His face was almost completely hidden by a long, shaggy mane of hair and a wild, tangled beard, but you could make out his eyes, glinting like black beetles under all the hair.
>
> From *Harry Potter and the Philosopher's Stone* by J K Rowling

This character seems quite frightening and imposing. This is because the writer has chosen to emphasise two of Hagrid's distinct qualities:
- his size: *twice as tall as a normal man*; *simply too big to be allowed*; *vast* and *giant*
- his connection with animals: *shaggy mane*; *baby dolphins*; *like black beetles*. The word *wild* is also repeated.

There is a clue in the description that Hagrid will not always be frightening. Look again at the final sentence of the second extract. His eyes are described as *glinting*. This word could suggest that there is also a smile lost under his enormous beard.

Hagrid can be very kind and he is always willing to put himself out to protect Harry Potter. There are two sides to his character, and **descriptions of his behaviour and speech help to form a more reliable impression of him.**

Behaviour

Read the extracts below from *Harry Potter and the Philosopher's Stone.*

> Harry looked up into the fierce, wild, shadowy face and saw that the beetle eyes were crinkled in a smile.
>
> * * * *
>
> Hagrid looked at Harry with warmth and respect blazing in his eyes...
>
> * * * *
>
> But he had finally gone too far. Hagrid seized his umbrella and whirled it over his head. "NEVER –" he thundered, "– INSULT – ALBUS – DUMBLEDORE – IN – FRONT – OF – ME!"
>
> He brought the umbrella swishing down through the air to point at Dudley – there was a flash of violet light, a sound like a firecracker, a sharp squeal and next second, Dudley was dancing on the spot with his hands clasped over his fat bottom, howling in pain. When he turned his back on them, Harry saw a curly pig's tail poking through a hole in his trousers.

These short extracts show how Hagrid's behaviour can change depending on whom he is dealing with.

Notice how the choice of **verbs** in the final extract indicates Hagrid's anger: *seized*, *whirled*, and *thundered*.

Speech

The way a character speaks can give the reader more **valuable clues** about him or her. As you read the next extract, think about:
- **what Hagrid says**
- **the way he speaks**
- **the way his speech is described**.

> 'Shouldn'ta lost me temper,' he said ruefully, 'but it didn't work anyway. Meant ter turn him into a pig, but I suppose he was so much like a pig anyway there wasn't much left ter do.'
>
> He cast a sideways look at Harry under his bushy eyebrows.
>
> 'Be grateful if yeh didn't mention that ter anyone at Hogwarts,' he said. 'I'm – er – not supposed ter do magic, strictly speakin'. I was allowed to do a bit ter follow yeh an' get yer letters to yeh an' stuff – one o' the reasons I was so keen ter take on the job –'

What he says

This shows that Hagrid isn't a bad person really – he knows he's done wrong, but he couldn't help himself. What he says about Dudley also shows that he is honest and won't stay quiet to spare someone's feelings.

The way he speaks

The way Hagrid's speech is written represents his **accent and dialect**. He doesn't speak in Standard English; his character would seem too formal if his speech was written in that form. Like a description of appearance, **the way a character speaks helps the reader to imagine them as a real person.**

The way his speech is described

Instead of always writing 'he said', the writer uses a range of **verbs** and **adverbs** to describe the way Hagrid speaks. This helps the reader to work out how a character feels when they are speaking:
- *he thundered* (verb) shows us that he is angry
- *he said ruefully* (adverb) shows that he is sorry about what he's done.

Sentence level

A **noun phrase** is a group of words with a noun as the central component. In fiction, the noun phrase is used to make writing more interesting and to add explanatory or descriptive detail. The other components of a noun phrase are usually **adjectives**.

The example below shows how J K Rowling uses a noun phrase to extend the description of Hagrid.

> Harry looked up into the **face** (noun)
>
> *Harry looked up into the **fierce, wild, shadowy face*** (noun phrase)

Perhaps it had something to do with living in a dark cupboard, but Harry had always been small and skinny for his age. He looked even smaller and skinnier than he really was because all he had to wear were old clothes of Dudley's and Dudley was about four times bigger than he was. Harry had a thin face, knobbly knees, black hair and bright-green eyes. He wore round glasses held together with a lot of Sellotape because of all the times Dudley had punched him on the nose. The only thing Harry liked about his own appearance was a very thin scar on his forehead which was shaped like a bolt of lightning.

Description of Harry Potter from *Harry Potter and the Philosopher's Stone* by J K Rowling

---

Progress Check

Read the extract above and answer these questions.
1 How is the reader supposed to feel about Harry?
2 Why are his glasses broken?
3 What details are emphasised most?
4 What is the most unusual thing about Harry's appearance?
5 What is the effect of mentioning the scar last?

1 We are supposed to feel sorry for him. 2 He has been punched by Dudley. 3 His size: he's very small and thin. 4 His lightning scar. 5 This makes it seem important.

2.2 Setting

Describing the setting and creating an atmosphere

Read the two extracts below. **In the first there is very little descriptive detail** and, as a result, there isn't a real sense of the setting or atmosphere. The second version is from David Almond's novel, *Kit's Wilderness* (the words and phrases that have been removed or changed in the first version are highlighted in the second). It is the first description of a very important setting for the first part of the novel, Askew's den. In this description Almond uses **a range of devices to create atmosphere and give the reader a real sense of the place**.

> In Stoneygate there was a wilderness. It was a space between the houses and the river, where the pit had been. That's where we played Askew's game. We used to gather at the school's gates after the bell had rung. We stood there. After five minutes, Bobby Carr told us it was time and he led us through the wilderness to Askew's den, a hole dug into the earth with doors across it as an entrance and a roof. The dog Jax waited for us there. When Jax began to growl, Askew opened one of the doors. He looked out at us and called us down.
>
> We went down the steps. We leaned against the walls. The floor was clay. Candles burned in the walls. There were some bones in a corner. There was a ditch where a fire burned in winter. The den was lined with dried mud. Askew had carved pictures of us all, of animals, of the dogs and cats we owned. He wrote into the walls the names of all of us who'd died in there. Allie Keenan sat across the den from me.

The original version, from *Kit's Wilderness* by David Almond:

> In Stoneygate there was a wilderness. It was an empty space between the houses and the river, where the ancient pit had been. That's where we played Askew's game, the game called Death. We used to gather at the school's gates after the bell had rung. We stood there whispering and giggling. After five minutes, Bobby Carr told us it was time and he led us through the wilderness to Askew's den, a deep hole dug into the earth with old doors slung across it as an entrance and a roof. The place was hidden from the school and from the houses of Stoneygate by the slope and by the tall grasses growing around it. The wild dog Jax waited for us there. When Jax began to growl, Askew drew one of the doors aside. He looked out at us, checked the faces, called us down.
>
> We stumbled one by one down the crumbling steps. We crouched against the walls. The floor was hard-packed clay. Candles burned in niches in the walls. There was a heap of bones in a corner. Askew told us they were human bones, discovered when he'd dug this place. There was a blackened ditch where a fire burned in winter. The den was lined with dried mud. Askew had carved pictures of us all, of animals, of the dogs and cats we owned, of the wild dog, Jax, of imagined monsters and demons, of the gates of Heaven and the snapping jaws of Hell. He wrote into the walls the names of all of us who'd died in there. My friend Allie Keenan sat across the den from me. The blankness in her eyes said: You're on your own down here

The devices used in this piece of writing are:
- descriptive detail
- particular vocabulary choices
- imagery
- sentence structure.

Vocabulary choices

Some of the vocabulary choices the author made are significant:
- *stumbled*, *crouched* – the **verb** choices give the impression that the characters feel nervous and uncertain in this setting
- *ancient*, *empty* – used alongside the word *wilderness*, these **adjectives** add to the impression of an unwelcoming and threatening place.

Descriptive detail

The additional detail that describes the den, its surroundings and the people who go there helps to make the setting seem more realistic.
- **The den** – the candles, the blackened ditch and the heap of 'human' bones give the den a frightening feel.
- **The surroundings** – the fact that the den is hidden from the school and the houses is significant. It reinforces the idea that the game of death is dangerous and probably forbidden. The den is detached from civilisation and this makes it more threatening.
- **Allie Keenan** – the description focuses more on place than people, but the additional detail about Allie is revealing. It suggests that people change their character when they are in the den. The narrator describes Allie as his friend, but in the sentence that follows her behaviour is distinctly unfriendly: *The blankness in her eyes said: You're on your own down here.*

Imagery

Imagery is used sparingly in this extract, but this makes it more effective.
- **Personification** – the author personifies Hell: *the gates of Heaven and the snapping jaws of Hell.* This image connects to the game of death, introduced earlier in the extract. It is intended to remind the characters and the reader of the possibilities that follow death. It also reminds the reader of the snapping jaws of *the wild dog Jax.*

Sentence structure

The comma in this sentence is a caesura.

A range of sentence structures is used in this extract.
- *That's where we played Askew's game, the game called death.* The structure of this sentence means that information about the subject of the game is delayed. Usually we would connect playing a game with fun. The phrase that follows the comma in this sentence reveals the more sinister nature of this particular game.
- Most of the sentences in the second paragraph are **short, simple sentences.**

- The sentence which begins *Askew had carved...* is much **longer** and has a **more complicated structure**, allowing the author to create a different effect.
- *Askew had carved pictures of us all, of animals, of the dogs and cats we owned, of the wild dog, Jax, of imagined monsters and demons, of the gates of Heaven and the snapping jaws of Hell.* This sentence places real domestic creatures alongside imagined demons and the frightening image of Hell. The list form of this sentence helps to **build up tension** as the images become less familiar and more frightening.

Progress Check

1 The children are described as *whispering and giggling* because they are:
a) amused b) nervous and excited c) bored.
2 Which word is always used to describe Askew's dog, Jax?
3 The setting and atmosphere of a piece of writing can only be created through the description of place. TRUE or FALSE?

1 b) nervous and excited   2 wild   3 false

2.3 Relationships

We all have relationships – with family, friends, teachers or work colleagues. To be believable, fictional characters must **develop relationships** within a text. The development of a relationship can often be the central element of the plot.

You should be able to:
- recognise how texts refer to and reflect the culture in which they were produced.

The extract below is taken from *A Kestrel for a Knave*, a novel written in 1968. This passage deals with the relationship between the main character, Billy Casper, and one of his teachers, Mr Sugden. As you read this extract think about:
- how you would describe the **relationship**
- how the writer **creates tension** between the two characters
- how the writing might **reflect the time in which it was produced**.

He thought this was funny, Billy didn't. So Sugden looked round for a more appreciative audience. But no one was listening. They faced up for a few more seconds, then Billy turned back to his peg. He undressed quickly, bending his pumps free of his heels and sliding them off without untying the laces. When he stood up the black soles of his socks stamped damp imprints on the dry floor, which developed into a haphazard set of footprints when he removed his socks and stepped around pulling his jeans down. His ankles and knees were ingrained with ancient dirt which seemed to belong to the pigmentation of his skin. His left leg sported a mud stripe, and both his knees were encrusted. The surfaces of these mobile crusts were hair-lined, and with every flexion of the knee these lines opened into frown-like furrows.

* * * *

While he worked on his ankles and heels Sugden stationed three boys at one end of the showers and moved to the other end, where the controls fed into the pipes on the wall...The blunt arrow was pointing to HOT. Sugden swung it back over WARM to COLD. For a few seconds there was no visible change in the temperature, and the red slice held steady, still dominating the dial. Then it began to recede, slowly at first, then swiftly, its share of the face diminishing rapidly.

The cold water made Billy gasp. He held out his hands as though testing for rain, then ran for the end. The three guards barred the exit.

'Hey up, shift! Let me out, you rotten dogs!' They held him easily so he swished back to the other end, yelling all the way along. Sugden pushed him in the chest as he clung his way round the corner.

'Got a sweat on, Casper?'

'Let me out, Sir. Let me come.'

'I thought you'd like a cooler after your exertions in goal.'

'I'm frozen!'

'Really?'

'Gi' o'er, Sir! It's not right!'

'And was it right when you let the last goal in?'

'I couldn't help it!'

'Rubbish, lad.'

Billy tried another rush. Sugden repelled it, so he tried the other end again. Every time he tried to escape the three boys bounced him back, stinging him with their snapping towels as he retreated. He tried manoeuvring the nozzles, but whichever way he twisted them the water still found him out. Until finally he gave up, and stood amongst them, tolerating the freezing spray in silence.

When Billy stopped yelling the other boys stopped laughing, and when time passed and no more was heard from him, their conversations began to peter out, and attention gradually focused on the showers. Until only a trio was left shouting into each other's faces, unaware that the volume of noise in the room had dropped. Suddenly they stopped, looked round embarrassed, then looked towards the showers with the rest of the boys.

The cold water had cooled the air, the steam had vanished, and the only sound that came from the showers was the beat of water behind the partition; a mesmeric beat which slowly drew the boys together on the drying area.

The boy guards began to look uneasy, and they looked across to their captain.

'Can we let him out now, Sir?'

'No!'

From A Kestrel for a Knave by Barry Hines

The **exclamation marks** show that Billy is in pain or discomfort.

Notice that the conversation is written as these people would really speak. **'Gi'o'er'** is how Billy would say 'Give over'. Billy doesn't speak in Standard English – this style of writing indicates Billy's dialect and accent.

The whole conversation shows that Mr Sugden is more powerful than Billy.

Mr Sugden's final comment shows that he thinks Billy is a liar.

The conversation isn't always written in complete sentences because we don't always speak in complete sentences.

How relationships can be depicted

The central feature of the relationship described in the extract from *A Kestrel for a Knave* is the **abuse of power**. In this relationship the teacher has all the power and the pupil has none. The physical bullying that goes on in the extract reflects the kind of behaviour that actually happened in some schools at the time the novel was written.

There are several ways that relationships and their development can be depicted in literature, including the use of:
- dialogue
- character behaviour
- other characters.

Dialogue

You can learn a lot about relationships between characters from **what they say to each other**. The annotations beside the text on page 23 explain many of the key features of the dialogue.
- Mr Sugden's **questions** show that he doesn't believe anything that Billy says.
- Mr Sugden's speech is quite **controlled** because he is in control of the exchange and the situation.
- Billy's **exclamations** show that he is more **emotional** and doesn't have any control over the situation.
- Mr Sugden's tone is **sarcastic**; this reflects his resentment about losing the football match.

Character behaviour

Mr Sugden behaves like a bully. He has **all the power** in the relationship and he exploits this:
- he thinks Billy's predicament is funny
- he gets the other boys on his side and uses them to punish and humiliate Billy
- he turns the shower to cold
- he pushes and shouts at Billy.

Billy has **no power** and he is unable to change the situation he finds himself in:
- he tries to escape but the other pupils prevent him from doing this
- he gives up and tolerates the freezing spray in silence.

Other characters
- Billy's poor relationship with the other boys makes it easier for Mr Sugden to pick on him.
- The other boys look up to Mr Sugden and are pleased to act as his guards.
- The way that the boys react at the end of the extract shows that even they think he has gone too far.
- The fact that the boys feel sorry for Billy makes the reader feel even more **sympathy** for him.

> **Word level**
>
> Lots of words in this extract end in **-tion**: *pigmentation*, *conversation*, *attention*, *partition*, *exertion*.
>
> There are many different ways to spell the **'shun'** ending sound. Use **-tion** when:
> - there is a long vowel sound before the 'shun' sound, e.g. **convers_a_tion**
> - there is a consonant before the 'shun' sound, e.g. **atten_tion**
> - there is a short 'i' sound before the 'shun' sound, e.g. **parti_tion**, except words with '**mission**', e.g. **permission**.

Progress Check

1 What gives the first clue that the boys are beginning to worry about Billy?
2 Find three words in the first paragraph that describe the mud and which have a similar meaning.
3 What is the effect of using all three words?

1 The other boys stopped laughing.   2 ingrained, encrusted, crusts
3 It emphasises how dirty Billy is.

2.4 Openings

The opening of a short story or the first chapter of a novel is **crucial**. The author has to get the reader's interest straightaway to convince them to keep on reading. It is important for the writer to get the right **balance** between giving enough information for the reader to decide whether they will enjoy the book, and keeping enough back for a few surprises along the way.

The following extract is a first chapter from a novel. As you read it, think about what makes it an effective opening chapter.

This is what Fliss dreamed the night before Year 7 went to Whitby.

She was walking on a road high above the sea. It was dark. She was alone. Waves were breaking at the foot of cliffs to her left, and further out, the moonlight made a silver path on the water.

In front of her was a house. It was a tall house looming blackly against the sky. There were many windows, all of them dark.

Fliss was afraid. She didn't want to go inside the house. She didn't even want to walk past but she had no control over her feet. They seemed to go by themselves, forcing her on.

She came to a gate. It was made of iron, worked into curly patterns. Near the top was a bit that was supposed to be a bird in flight – a seagull perhaps – but the gate had been painted black, and the paint had run and hardened into little stalactites along the bird's wings, making it look like a bat.

The gate opened by itself, and as she went through Fliss heard a voice that whispered, 'The Gate of Fate.' She was drawn along a short pathway and up some stone steps to the front door, which also opened by itself. 'The Keep of Sleep,' whispered the voice.

The door closed silently behind her. Moonlight shone coldly through a stained-glass panel into a gloomy hallway. At the far end were stairs that went up into blackness. She didn't want to climb that stairway but her feet drew her along the hallway and up.

She came to a landing with doors. The stairs took a turn and went on up. As Fliss climbed, it grew colder. There was another landing, more doors and another turn in the stairs. Upward to a third landing, then a fourth, and then there were no more stairs. She was at the top of the house. There were four doors, each with a number. 10. 11. 12. 13. As she read the numbers, door thirteen swung inward with a squeal. 'No!' she whispered, but it was no use. Her feet carried her over the threshold and the voice hissed, 'The Room of Doom.'

In the room was a table. On the table stood a long, pale box. Fliss thought she knew what it was. It filled her with horror, and she whimpered helplessly as her feet drew her towards it. When she was close she saw a shape in the box and there was a smell like damp earth. When she was very close the voice whispered, 'The Bed of Dread,' and then the shape sat up and reached out for her and she screamed. Her screams woke her and she lay damp and trembling in her bed.

Her mother came and switched on the light and looked down at her. 'What is it, Felicity? I thought I heard you scream.'

Fliss nodded. 'I had a dream, Mum. A nightmare.'

'Poor Fliss.' Her mother sat down on the bed and stroked her hair. 'It's all the excitement, I expect, thinking about going away tomorrow.' She smiled. 'Try to go back to sleep, dear. You've a long day ahead you.'

Fliss clutched her mother's arm. 'I don't want to go, Mum.'

'What?'

'I don't want to go. I want to drop out of the trip.'

'But why – not just because of a silly dream, surely?'

'Well, yes, I suppose so, Mum. It was about Whitby, I think. A house by the sea.'

'A house?'

'Yes.' She shivered, remembering. 'I was in this house and something horrible was after me. Can I drop out, Mum?'

Her mother sighed. 'I suppose you could, Felicity, if you're as upset as all that. I could ring Mrs Evans first thing, tell her not to expect you, but you might feel differently in the morning.' She smiled. 'Daylight makes us forget our dreams, or else they seem funny – even the scary ones. Let's decide in the morning, eh?'

Fliss smiled wanly 'OK.' She knew she wouldn't forget her dream, and that it would never seem funny. But it was all right. She was in control of her feet (she wiggled them under the covers to make sure), and they weren't going to take her anywhere she didn't want to go.

From *Room 13* by Robert Swindells

Examining the story

What happens?

Start by thinking about what actually happens in the extract.
- Fliss **dreams** about a strange house by the sea.
- Fliss **goes into** Room 13.
- Fliss **sees a strange box** with someone or something in it.
- Fliss **wakes up** from her nightmare.
- Her **mum comforts her**, but Fliss decides she doesn't want to go to Whitby.

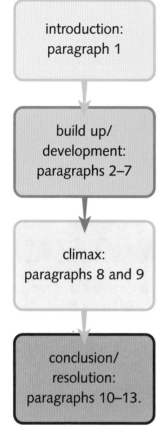

introduction:
paragraph 1

build up/
development:
paragraphs 2–7

climax:
paragraphs 8 and 9

conclusion/
resolution:
paragraphs 10–13.

Structure of the story

Most stories follow a similar structure. The whole novel follows this structure, but the opening chapter on page 26 also follows the same structure, **as shown in the flow diagram on the left.**

However, the first chapter of the novel only provides a short-term resolution. There are many questions left unanswered, and this is what makes people want to read on.

Main character

Fliss is the main character in both the story and in this first chapter. We learn quite a lot about her and what to expect from her as the novel progresses:

- she has a vivid imagination
- she is frightened by the dream: *then the shape sat up and reached out for her and she screamed. Her screams woke her and she lay damp and trembling in her bed.*
- she doesn't want to go on the school trip
- she likes to be in control of what she is doing: *She was in control of her feet (she wiggled them under the covers to make sure), and they weren't going to take her anywhere she didn't want to go.*
- she is not easily convinced by her mum's explanation.

Setting

The setting for this chapter is mainly within Fliss's dream. It is set in an old house by the sea at night time. Fliss is convinced that her dream was about Whitby – this is important as it **gives us a clue** that the rest of the story will be set in Whitby. It also hints that the frightening setting of her dream will be revisited.

There are a number of elements that make the setting seem frightening:

- **circumstances**: it is dark and she is alone
- **descriptions**: a tall house *looming blackly*; *Moonlight shone coldly ... into a gloomy hallway*; stairs that went up into *blackness*
- **choice of adjectives**: *dark, alone, afraid, black, gloomy*.

The adjectives help to create the frightening atmosphere/setting. They add detail, helping the reader to imagine what the house looked like.

What next?

Fliss tells her mum that she isn't going to Whitby with the rest of Year 7, but everything about the opening chapter suggests that she will go. Fliss is obviously the main character and her dream is given so much prominence in this chapter that it must be important to the rest of the story. We are kept guessing as to why her dream is so important and the only way to find out is to read the rest of the novel. This kind of **hook** is a good way to open a novel.

> **Word level**
>
> **Adverbs:** an adverb is a describing word. It describes how a verb is done. Many adverbs end in **-ly**. Often, an adverb can be formed by adding **-ly** to an adjective: black**ly**, cold**ly**, silent**ly**.

Progress Check

1 Which room does Fliss go into in her dream?
2 What is Fliss's full name?
3 What technique is used when the whispering voice speaks, *Bed of dread...* and so on?

1 room 13   2 Felicity   3 rhyme

2.5 Shakespeare

Themes

All of Shakespeare's plays explore particular ideas or issues that recur and develop as the play progresses. These ideas and issues are known as the **themes** of the play.

Shakespeare's plays cover the same themes as any modern piece of writing:

- love
- jealousy
- ambition

- family conflicts
- murder and intrigue
- revenge.

When you are studying a Shakespeare play, you should think about what the themes are and how they are revealed and developed.

Structure

Most plays follow a similar pattern of development, and Shakespeare's plays are no exception.

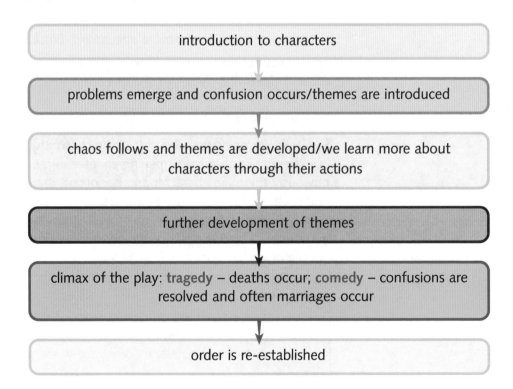

> introduction to characters

> problems emerge and confusion occurs/themes are introduced

> chaos follows and themes are developed/we learn more about characters through their actions

> further development of themes

> climax of the play: **tragedy** – deaths occur; **comedy** – confusions are resolved and often marriages occur

> order is re-established

Understanding Shakespeare's language

Key Point

Hearing Shakespeare's language read aloud helps you to understand the meaning. Try to see a live performance or a video version of the play you are studying.

Rhyme and rhythm

There are different types of rhyme and rhythm in Shakespeare's plays.

- **Blank verse** – this is unrhymed lines of **iambic pentameter** (10 syllables alternately unstressed and stressed). Shakespeare wrote his plays in blank verse because it is versatile, it is not restricted by rhyme and it is the closest to the **natural rhythms of speech**. This makes it easy to create different moods, such as anger, love, and so on.

- **Iambic pentameter** – this term describes the number of **syllables** and **stresses** in a line, which is known as the **meter**. A **foot** is a pair of syllables. An iambic foot is an unstressed syllable followed by a stressed syllable. **There are five iambic feet in iambic pentameter.** Look at the example below, from Shakespeare's *Henry V* Act 1, scene 1, lines 67–69:

> Canterbury:
> It <u>must</u> / be <u>so</u>, / for <u>mir</u> / acles / are <u>ceas'd,</u>
> And <u>there</u> / fore <u>we</u> / must <u>needs</u> / ad<u>mit</u> / the <u>means</u>,
> How <u>things</u> / are <u>per</u> / fected./

- **Rhyming couplets** – sometimes Shakespeare wrote in different styles for contrast. More **formal** and **traditional characters** making important speeches sometimes speak in rhyming couplets (the lines rhyme in pairs). Because of the constraint of finding rhymes, there is less movement and freedom in these speeches. This reflects the characters' formality. Look at the example below, from Shakespeare's *Much Ado About Nothing* Act 3, scene 1, lines 105–106:

> Hero:
> If it prove so, then loving goes by haps,
> Some Cupid kills with arrows, some with traps.

Sometimes Shakespeare used a rhyming couplet to **round off** an important speech or scene. He also used rhyming couplets to **create** a particular kind of **atmosphere** or to present a character or event in a different way. The witches in *Macbeth* (Act 1, scene 1, lines 1–2) speak in rhyming couplets, and Shakespeare doesn't use iambic pentameter for their speeches.

> When shall we three meet again
> In thunder, lightning or in rain?

- **Prose** – the 'low characters', servants for example, speak in prose rather than verse. This reflects that they have less education and their subject matter is often low or coarse.

> **Trinculo:** I shall laugh myself to death at this puppy headed monster. A most scurvy monster: I could find in my heart to beat him –
>
> From Shakespeare's *The Tempest* Act 2, scene 2 lines 140–142

> **Porter:** Marry, sir, nose-painting, sleep, and urine.
>
> From Shakespeare's *Macbeth* Act 2, scene 3, line 27

Other characters sometimes speak in prose rather than verse. The important thing to remember is that Shakespeare always used blank verse, rhymed verse and prose for a particular reason.

How to read Shakespeare aloud

Key Point

If you are reading Shakespeare aloud, try to read to the punctuation. This will help with the sense of what you are reading.

Shakespeare's language is always much easier to understand when it is read well. Follow these tips.
- **Read to the punctuation** – if there is no punctuation at the end of a line then read straight through to the next line.
- **Don't rush** – speak clearly and think about what you are saying.
- **Words ending in 'd or -ed** – if a word is spelt 'd, e.g. **accus'd**, you pronounce it as we would say **accused**. However, if it is spelt **accused** in the text you pronounce the -ed as a separate syllable: **accuse-ed**.
- **Think about the tone of voice you should use.**
- **Think about what your character would do when saying the lines.**
- **Emphasise the words you think are most important** – the natural stresses of iambic pentameter should help you to do this.

Word level

Since Shakespeare's time there have been many changes to the English language, both in the way it is written and in the way it is spoken. The table on page 31 shows you the Shakespearian and modern English forms of some common words.

Thee.. thou.. who?	
Shakespeare	Modern English
art	are
hadst	had
hence	here
ill	bad
o'er	over
thee	you
thou	you used with someone very close to you or as an insult
you	you a more distant way of speaking to someone
thy	your
whence	where (from)
wither	where (to)
wouldst	would

Progress Check

1 Is the climax of a tragedy most likely to be a death or a marriage?

2 Does blank verse have 8, 10 or 12 syllables in each line?

3 The word *turn'd* should be pronounced with *-ed* as an extra syllable. TRUE or FALSE?

1. a death 2. ten 3. false

Shakespeare's language – *Macbeth*

Key Point

Soliloquy – a character is alone on stage and speaks his or her thoughts aloud. Playwrights use this device to give the audience important information about the character and their motives that other characters in the play are unaware of.

You should be able to:

● analyse the language, form and dramatic impact of scenes and plays by published dramatists.

The story so far: the witches have predicted that Macbeth will be King; he and his wife have planned to murder King Duncan. In the following soliloquy, Macbeth is having second thoughts.

He's here in **double trust**;
First as I am **his kinsman** and his **subject**,
Strong both against the deed; then as **his host**,
Who should against his murderer shut the door,   15
Not bear the knife myself. Besides this Duncan
Hath borne his faculties so **meek**, hath been
So **clear** in his great office, that his virtues
Will plead like angels, **trumpet-tongued** against

> The **deep damnation** of his **taking-off** 20
> And pity, like a **naked newborn babe**
> striding the blast, or heaven's cherubin horsed
> Upon the sightless couriers of the air,
> Shall blow **the horrid deed** in every eye,
> That tears shall drown the wind. I have no spur 25
> To prick the sides of my intent, but only
> Vaulting ambition which o'erleaps itself
> and falls on th'other –
>
> *Macbeth* Act 1, scene 7, lines 12–28

Lines 12–16
- The phrase *double trust* emphasises that Macbeth would be breaking Duncan's trust twice. He sets out the reasons logically:
  1a he is his *kinsman* (relative)
  1b he is a trusted *subject*
  2 Duncan is a guest in Macbeth's house, so he should protect him, not plan to kill him.
- Macbeth presents himself with a **well-reasoned argument** against the murder plan.

Lines 16–18
- These lines are more **emotive**. Macbeth reminds himself of all Duncan's qualities. Words like *meek* and *clear* are used to show that Duncan is virtuous and without sin.

Line 20
- Duncan's goodness is **contrasted** with the *deep damnation* of the act of murder. This is a direct comparison of the spiritual state of the two men, Duncan and Macbeth, his killer. Macbeth realises that he would be damned for eternity for such a sinful act.

Lines 21–25
- He uses images of innocence and purity – the **new born baby** and the **cherubin** (the highest order of angels) – as the messengers of Duncan's death. He imagines that the winds will be drowned with tears. This emphasises the scale of public mourning for the death of such a king.

Lines 25–28
- In comparison with all the reasons not to kill Duncan, Macbeth's only reason to carry out the murder is his ambition. He **compares** his ambition to a horse that tries to jump too high and falls on the other side of the fence. Macbeth thinks that if he gives in to ambition, he will fail in the end.
- Alliteration is used for emphasis in this speech: *trumpet-tongued*, *deep damnation*, *naked newborn babe*.

Euphemism – a mild or inoffensive way of expressing something unpleasant, frightening or offensive.

In this speech Macbeth lists all the reasons why he shouldn't murder Duncan. Throughout the soliloquy he uses **euphemisms** for the murder, e.g. *bear the knife*, *his taking-off*, *horrid deed*. This shows that Macbeth is reluctant to think about the brutality of the act of murder. He is trying to avoid the reality of the situation and cannot face up to the evil nature of the plan that he and his wife have made.

Shakespeare's language – *Much Ado About Nothing*

Don John convinces Claudio and Don Pedro that Hero has been unfaithful before the wedding night. He tells them that he can show them evidence of her disloyalty if they go with him.

DON JOHN	I came hither to tell you, and circumstances shortened (for she has been too long a-talking of), the lady is disloyal.
CLAUDIO	Who Hero?
DON JOHN	Even she, Leonato's Hero, your Hero, every man's Hero.
CLAUDIO	Disloyal?
DON JOHN	The word is too good to paint out her wickedness, I could say she were worse, think you of a worse title, and I will fit her to it: wonder not till further warrant: go but with me tonight, you shall see her chamber window entered, even the night before her wedding day: if you love her, then tomorrow wed her: but it would better fit your honour to change your mind.
CLAUDIO	May this be so?
DON PEDRO	I will not think it.
DON JOHN	If you dare not trust that you see, confess not that you know: if you will follow me, I will show you enough: and when you have seen more, and heard more, proceed accordingly.
CLAUDIO	If I see anything tonight, why I should not marry her tomorrow in the congregation, where I should wed, there will I shame her.
DON PEDRO	And as I wooed for thee to obtain her, I will join with thee, to disgrace her.
DON JOHN	I will disparage her no farther, till you are my witnesses: bear it coldly but till midnight, and let the issue show itself.
DON PEDRO	Oh day untowardly turned!
CLAUDIO	Oh mischief strangely thwarting!
DON JOHN	Oh plague right well prevented! So will you say, when you have seen the sequel.

Much Ado About Nothing Act 3, scene 2, lines 75–100

Lines 75–79
● Hero's name is repeated four times in this section. This is done to show that there can be no misunderstanding about who has been disloyal (even though there clearly is a misunderstanding); to emphasise how important Hero is to Claudio and her father; most importantly, Don John uses the final repetition to suggest that she is unfaithful and has slept with many men *every man's Hero*.

Lines 80–85
● Don John tries to emphasise her wrongdoing by suggesting that the word 'disloyal' is not strong enough to show the full scale of her wickedness. He says he could list crimes to fit her to the worst title they can think of. Alliteration on w is used to link her *wickedness* with the scene of her supposed crime the *chamber window* and with the planned *wedding*.

Lines 88–90
● Don John tries to create a sense of truth around his allegations by saying that if they are not prepared to trust the evidence of their own eyes, then they can never say that they know anything. He claims that if they follow him they will see and hear enough evidence to know what to do.

Lines 91–94
- Claudio and Don Pedro create patterns in the way they speak that contrast what **should** or **has** happened with what **will** happen. Shakespeare does this to show that they are almost convinced by Don John before they have seen anything. They are all thinking the same way which is to join together to disgrace Hero.

Lines 95–96
- Don John cleverly **avoids** being accused of turning them against Hero by stepping back and saying he won't say any more about her until they have seen the evidence for themselves.

Lines 97–100
- The patterns of language and **sentence structure** in the final lines of the scene show that all three men are united against Hero. Each man's final line is an **exclamation**. Whilst Claudio and Don Pedro look at the negative, Don John suggests it's **positive** as they will find Hero out in time to stop the wedding.

Shakespeare's language – *Richard III*

King Edward explains that the company have been making their peace together and invites Richard to join them in friendship. Richard expresses peace and goodwill to everyone present.

KING EDWARD	Happy indeed, as we have spent the day.
	Gloucester, we have done **deeds of charity**,
	Made **peace of enmity, fair love of hate,**
	Between these swelling, wrong-incensèd peers.
RICHARD	A blessed labour, my most sovereign lord.
	Among this **princely heap**, if any here
	By **false intelligence** or **wrong surmise**
	Hold me a foe; if I **unwillingly, or in my rage**
	Have aught committed that is hardly borne
	To any in this presence, I **desire**
	To reconcile me to his friendly peace.
	'Tis death to me to be at enmity;
	I **hate** it and **desire** all good men's **love**.

Richard III Act 2, scene 1, lines 49–61

Lines 49–52
- King Edward **contrasts** peace and hatred throughout this speech to emphasise how they have put any bad feeling behind them and are looking forward to friendship; *deeds of charity* and *peace* have replaced *enmity*, and *fair love* has replaced *hate*.

Lines 53–59
- Richard immediately picks up the **tone** of reconciliation and claims to be upset at the idea of angering any of the important company *princely heap*. He suggests that any offence he has caused must be the product of incorrect information *false intelligence* or drawing the wrong conclusions *wrong surmise*. He says that if he has offended anyone he will have done it *unwillingly, or in my rage*. He emphasises his intention to make peace by using the word *desire* to show how important it is.

Lines 60–61
- He further emphasises his desire for peace by suggesting he would rather die than have enemies **tis death to me to be at enmity**. In his next line he uses three strong words **hate**, **desire** and **love** to show the importance of peace.

Shakespeare's language – *The Tempest*

Caliban curses Prospero and says that the spirits under Prospero's control torment him for every little thing he does wrong.

> CALIBAN All the **infections** that the sun sucks up
> From **bogs, fens, flats**, on Prosper fall, and make him
> By **inch-meal a disease**. His spirits hear me,
> And yet I needs must curse. But they'll nor **pinch**,
> **Fright me** with urchin-shows, **pitch me i'th'mire**,
> Nor **lead me like a firebrand in the dark**
> **Out of my way**, unless he bid 'em; but
> For every **trifle** are they set upon me,
> Sometime like apes, that mow and chatter at me
> And after **bite me**; then like hedgehogs, which
> Lie tumbling in my barefoot way and **mount**
> **Their pricks at my footfall**; sometime am I
> All wound with adders, who with cloven tongues
> Do hiss me into madness.
>
> *The Tempest* Act 2, scene 2, lines 1–14

Lines 1–3
- Caliban's hatred is emphasised by the **listing device** used in line two; he wants to draw up 'infections' from as many places as he can *bogs, fens, flats*. Rather than wishing Prospero to suffer from a disease, he wants to *make him ... a disease*. This together with the idea of him being consumed by it inch by inch *by inch-meal*, suggests that Caliban enjoys the idea of Prospero being made to suffer as much as possible.

Lines 4–7
- Caliban begins to list all the terrible things that Prospero tells his spirit to do to him. At first the emphasis is on mental rather than physical cruelty. They confuse him, frighten him and lead him astray.

Line 8
- The word *trifle* is used to emphasise the fact that he feels he is punished for very minor offences.

Lines 9–14
- The **effect** of these lines is to **build up** the range of tortures used and **reflect** the fact that Caliban's rage and fear are **building up** under this relentless torment. This list of torments focuses more on the physical dangers he faces – being bitten by apes, pricked by hedgehogs and crushed by adders. The overall effect is revisited in the final line of this section when Caliban claims to be *hiss[ed] into madness*.

Practice test questions

The following questions will help you to prepare for the Optional Tests in Years 7 and 8. Read the extract below and answer the questions that follow.

> We had no torch. The light that came through the chinks in the boards was pale and weak. We blundered through the dark.
>
> We held hands and stretched our free hands out in front us. We walked into the wall. We caught our toes on loose floorboards. We stumbled as we climbed the stairs. We shuffled across the first landing. We felt for the handle of the door to the room where we thought we'd left Skellig. We inched the door open. We whispered, 'Skellig! Skellig!' No answer. We moved forward carefully, arms outstretched, feeling forward with our feet before we took each step. Our breath was fast, shallow, trembly. My heart was thundering. I opened my eyes wide, glared into the dark, seeking the shape of his body on the floor. Nothing there, just the blankets, the pillow, the plastic dish, the beer bottle rolling away from my stumbling feet.
>
> 'Where is he?' whispered Mina.
>
> 'Skellig,' we whispered. 'Skellig! Skellig!'
>
> We turned back to the landing again, we stumbled up the next flight of stairs, we opened many doors, we stared past them into pitch black rooms, we whispered his name, we heard nothing but our own breath, our own uncertain feet, his name echoing back to us from bare floorboards and bare walls, we turned back to the landing again, we stumbled up the next flight of stairs.
>
> From *Skellig* by David Almond

1 Find **three** examples of **verbs** used to describe the characters' movement. What effect do these words have? [2]

2 Describe the structure of the final sentence. Why is this effective? [3]

3 What techniques are used to create a feeling of fear and tension in this extract? [5]

The following questions will help you prepare for SATs in Year 9. The time allowance given below is for one question. In the SAT exams there will be **one question** to answer on the two extracts from the set scenes you have studied. During your preparation, try to answer all of these questions.

The reading section of the Shakespeare paper assesses:
● your understanding of the scenes and the whole play you have studied.
● your understanding of and response to characters, relationships and plot development.

Remember, you must support your opinions with relevant quotations and textual evidence.

These mock exam questions are very general so that they can be applied to any combination of scenes from the set plays: Macbeth, Richard III, Much Ado About Nothing and The Tempest. Try to answer these questions for your specified scenes.

Time: 45 minutes

Assessment: AT2

Staging

1 **You are the director of the play. Write detailed instructions for how each of the main characters should be played in these scenes.**

Think about:
- how they should move
- how they should behave
- how they should speak
- what their relationships should be with other characters.

Literary criticism

Choose the most appropriate question for your scenes from the list below.

2 **How is the atmosphere created or changed in these scenes?**

Think about:
- How the characters would behave
- What the main characters would be thinking – are they hiding anything?
- What has just happened or is about to happen.

3 **Comment on the behaviour of the main character(s) in these scenes.**

Think about:
- How they behave towards other characters
- The language that they use
- What is happening in each scene.

4 **How are relationships developed in these scenes?**

Think about:
- The way the characters behave towards each other
- The language they use
- Have the events of the play affected these characters directly?

5 **Why are the scenes important to the play's development?**

Think about:
- What happens before and after these scenes
- The way the main characters behave in these scenes.

6 **The main character(s) is/are under pressure in these scenes. How do they respond to that pressure?**

Think about:
- What they do
- The language they use
- How their behaviour may have changed
- What happens next.

Time: 45 minutes
Assessment: AT2 reading

3 Reading poetry

After studying this section you should be able to:

- understand poetry that tells a story
- comment on the use of imagery in poetry
- comment on the structure of a poem
- comment on and understand pre-1914 poetry
- compare poems on the same theme

To achieve the following National Curriculum levels you need to

Level 4
- understand what the poem is about
- understand the **ideas and feelings** in the poem

Level 5
- begin to look for layers of **meaning** beneath the surface of the text
- notice the effects of **particular words and phrases**

Level 6
- comment on the effective use of words and phrases and particular **devices of language**
- locate and comment on the **use of imagery**

Level 7
- comment on the **structure of the poem**
- trace development within a poem
- give a **personal response** to the poem and what you think the poet has achieved

3.1 Poetry that tells a story

Understanding poetry

You shouldn't expect to understand everything about a poem after a first reading; it will be packed full of emotions, ideas and images. Reading a poem involves detective work – you have to look closely under the surface for clues.

Try reading a poem through **three times**, each time looking for a different set of clues:

- **first reading** – the general meaning and story line of the poem (if it has one)
- **second reading** – feelings and emotions contained in the poem
- **third reading** – interesting images contained in the poem.

Ballads

A **ballad** is a poem that **tells a story**. It is a **traditional** kind of poetry that began as an oral storytelling form. The stories were told in **rhyme** so that they were easier to remember without being written down. Ballads still follow a lot of the same conventions now:

- tell a story
- strong, regular rhythm and rhyme
- repeated lines or refrains (**chorus**)
- often have a moral.

'What Has Happened to Lulu?' by Charles Causley

What has happened to Lulu, mother?
  What has happened to Lu?
There's **nothing in her bed** but an old rag doll
And by its side a shoe.

Why is her **window wide**, mother,
  The curtain flapping free,
And only a circle on the dusty shelf
  Where her **money-box** used to be?

Why do you turn your head, mother,
  And why do the tear-drops fall?
And why do you crumple that **note** on the fire
  And say it is nothing at all?

I woke to hear voices late last night,
  I heard **an engine roar**,
Why do you tell me the things I heard
  Were a dream and nothing more?

I heard somebody **cry**, mother,
  In anger or in pain,
But now I ask you why, mother,
  You say it was a gust of rain.

Why do you **wander about** as though
  You don't know what to do?
What has happened to Lulu, mother?
  What has happened to Lu?

Key Point

When you study a new poem you should read it three times.
Look for:
- the general meaning
- feelings and emotions
- interesting images.

The story

The way the poem 'What has happened to Lulu?' is written allows the reader to piece the story together stanza by stanza. There is a **clue** in each one:

1 empty bed
2 open window and missing money-box
3 note
4 engine roar late at night
5 crying
6 mum distracted.

The child's sister has run away. Mother doesn't want to talk about it and the child is trying to find out what happened.

Solving a mystery

The next poem only tells part of a story, it **reveals a mystery**. The poem raises as many questions as it answers. As you read the poem, think about the **questions** that it raises and the information that isn't supplied.

'The Way Through the Woods'
by Rudyard Kipling

They shut the road through the woods
Seventy years ago.
Weather and rain have undone it again,
And now you would never know
There was once a road through the woods
Before they planted the trees.
It is underneath the coppice and heath
And the thin anemones.
Only the keeper sees
That, where the ring-dove broods,
And the badgers roll at ease,
There was once a road through the woods.

Yet, if you enter the woods
Of a summer evening late,
When the night-air cools on the trout-ringed pools
Where the otter whistles his mate,
(They fear not men in the woods,
Because they see so few.)
You will hear the beat of a horse's feet,
And the swish of a skirt in the dew,
Steadily cantering through
The misty solitudes,
As though they perfectly knew
The old lost road through the woods...
But there is no road through the woods.

The following questions are raised in the poem.
- **Why** did 'they' shut the road?
- **Who** are 'they'?
- **Why** do so few men go into the woods?
- **Who** does the skirt that swishes belong to?

Progress Check

1 Which lines of the first poem are repeated?
2 Is the rhyme scheme of the second poem **regular** or **irregular**?
3 Which ballad feature does the second poem have?

1 lines 1 and 2   2 regular   3 repeated lines

3.2 Imagery

You should be able to:

● recognise how writers' language choices can enhance meaning, e.g. repetition, emotive vocabulary, varied sentence structure or line length, sound effects.

Read the poem printed below. It makes use of one particular kind of imagery. Can you work out what it is? You could use the **glossary** on pages 153–156 to help you.

'City Jungle' by Pie Corbett

Rain splinters town.

Lizard cars cruise by;
their radiators grin.

Thin headlights stare –
shop doorways keep
their mouths shut.

At the roadside
hunched houses cough.
Newspapers shuffle by,
hands in their pockets.
The gutter gargles.

A motorbike snarls;
dustbins flinch.

Streetlights bare
their yellow teeth.
The motorway's cat-black tongue
lashes across
the glistening back
of the tarmac night.

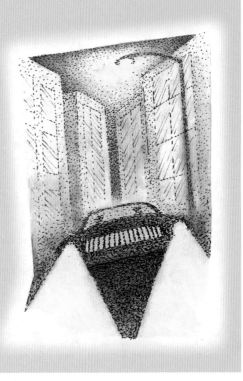

Personification

Throughout this poem, the poet uses **personification** to bring the city he describes to life.

Most of the personification is created through the poet's choice of **verbs** – *grin, stare, flinch, cough*. The objects described perform human or animal actions and this makes them appear to be living creatures.

The poet also uses some carefully chosen **nouns** to add to the effect of personification. The shop doorways become *mouths* in shop front faces and the newspapers put their *hands* in their *pockets*.

Key Point

● **Personification** is an image that brings an inanimate object to life by giving it human qualities.
● **Alliteration** is the term for a group of words that all begin with the same letter.

Painting pictures with words

The poet uses personification to create a **threatening atmosphere**. The city is described at night when, in the darkness, inanimate objects come to life and rule the city.

The cars and motorbikes are presented as arrogant and aggressive, like bullies. The dustbins, which rattle because of the vibrations made by the motorbike's engine, become the innocent victims of the bullies.

A motorbike snarls;
Dustbins flinch.

The phrase **hunched houses** makes you think of terraced houses very close together. The fact that they are **coughing** suggests that they are damp and cold; their chimneys could be smoking.

The description of the newspapers is very effective. These newspapers have been read and thrown away and are blowing around in the wind. The way the poet describes them makes them sound like people keeping their heads down, trying to get home and ignoring the bullies.

Newspapers shuffle by,
Hands in their pockets.

Progress Check

1 What technique is used in the lines *hunched houses cough* and *The gutter gargles*?

2 How would you describe the structure of the poem? a) It has a regular rhythm and rhyme scheme. b) It is written in free verse (no regular rhythm or rhyme scheme).

3 Why is the title of the poem effective?

1 alliteration   2 free verse   3 It makes the city sound alive, dangerous and unfamiliar.

Simile and metaphor

Read the two poems that follow. Can you identify the **simile** and the **metaphor**?

From 'Night of the Scorpion' by Nissim Ezekiel

I remember the night my mother
was stung by a scorpion. Ten hours
of steady rain had driven him
to crawl beneath a sack of rice.
Parting with his poison – flash
of diabolic tail in the dark room
he risked the rain again.
The peasants came like swarms of flies
and buzzed the name of God a hundred times
to paralyse the Evil One.

From 'Valentine' by Carol Ann Duffy

Not a red rose or a satin heart.

I give you an onion.
It is a moon wrapped in brown paper.

Key Point
Don't confuse similes and metaphors. A **simile** is a comparison of two objects using the words **like** or **as**. A **metaphor** states that one object **is** another object, without making a **comparison**.

Similes

The highlighted section of **'Night of the Scorpion'** is a **simile**. The poet describes his peasant neighbours as being **like flies** because there are so many of them. It also suggests that, even though they probably wanted to help, they were irritating him and getting in the way. The poet continues the image by describing the way they speak as *buzzing*.

Metaphors

The highlighted section of **'Valentine'** is a **metaphor**. This is effective because it's an unusual way to describe an onion, but when you think carefully about the physical qualities of an onion it makes perfect sense. Think about the colour and texture of an onion skin – it is just like brown paper. The onion itself is round, it reflects light and it is the same colour as the moon.

Making an unusual connection between the moon and an onion is also effective because the poem is about an unusual gift. It is about giving an onion as a valentine gift instead of a traditional card or roses.

Traditionally, the moon and moonlight are connected to romance and love – describing the onion in this way connects it to the subject of the poem.

Progress Check

1 Is a comparison of two different objects or ideas using the words *like* or *as* a **simile** or a **metaphor**.
2 **Personification** is a type of metaphor. TRUE or FALSE?
3 Find an example of alliteration in 'Night of the Scorpion'.

1 simile   2 true   3 lines 2, 5, 6 and 7

3.3 Structure

You should be able to:

● explore how form contributes to meaning in poems from different times and cultures.

The structure of a poem is very important. A writer can create many different effects with rhyme, rhythm, shape, line length and stanza form. In the Japanese poetry form, **haiku**, structure is the most important feature.

The structure of a haiku poem is always the same:
● **three lines**
● **first line five syllables**
● **second line seven syllables**
● **final line five syllables.**

This kind of structure doesn't allow for expansive imagery; instead, a brief, striking impression of nature is created.

Over the wintry
forest, winds howl in a rage
with no leaves to blow.

Studying the structure of a poem

The next poem is about a young boy (the poet) interested in nature, particularly frogspawn; he collects it and watches it grow. One day, the frogs frighten him and he imagines that they are going to attack him. He runs away, and this ends his interest in nature.

When you read this poem, you should pay particular attention to the **structure**. Some of the important features have been highlighted for you.

'Death of a Naturalist'
by Seamus Heaney

All year the flax-dam festered in the heart
Of the townland; green and heavy headed
Flax had rotted there, weighted down by huge sods.
Daily it sweltered in the punishing sun.
Bubbles gargled delicately, bluebottles
Wove a strong gauze of sound around the smell.
There were dragon-flies, spotted butterflies,
But best of all was the warm thick slobber
Of frogspawn that grew like clotted water
In the shade of the banks. Here, every spring
I would fill jampotsful of the jellied
Specks to range on window-sills at home,
On shelves at school, and wait and watch until
The fattening dots burst into nimble-
Swimming tadpoles. Miss Walls would tell us how
The daddy frog was called a bullfrog
And how he croaked and how the mammy frog
Laid hundreds of little eggs and this was
Frogspawn. You could tell the weather by frogs too
For they were yellow in the sun and brown
In rain.

Then one hot day when fields were rank
With cowdung in the grass and angry frogs
Invaded the flax-dam; I ducked through hedges
To a coarse croaking that I had not heard
Before. The air was thick with a bass chorus.
Right down the dam gross-bellied frogs were cocked
On sods; their loose necks pulsed like sails. Some hopped:
The slap and plop were obscene threats. Some sat
Poised like mud grenades, their blunt heads farting.
I sickened, turned, and ran. The great slime kings
Were gathered there for vengeance and I knew
That if I dipped my hand the spawn would clutch it.

time

enjambment

long sentence

time

short sentence

Rhyme, rhythm and stanza length

The poem **doesn't rhyme**, but as many of the lines are intended to flow from one to the next it doesn't need to.

The poem does have a **regular rhythm** and syllabic pattern. Most lines in the poem have ten syllables (some have eleven or twelve). Despite this regularity, the poem does speed up and slow down as you read it. The poet has used punctuation to control the speed of the poem.

The poem is **written in two stanzas**. Each stanza deals with very different emotions. The first clearly deals with the boy's enjoyment of nature and collecting frogspawn, whilst the second is full of bitter disappointment and fear. The second stanza is shorter than the first. This is because there is less lyrical and 'romantic' description – it is more matter-of-fact. It also represents the sudden death of his interest in nature.

Time

The poem is ordered by reference to time. In the first stanza all the times are general: *All year, every spring*. The first stanza describes a general interest in nature. It also shows that the collecting of frogspawn is something he does every year and that he is very familiar with the area he describes, having visited it often: *Daily it sweltered....*

The reference to time in the second stanza is a signpost for the move from **general** enjoyment to a **specific event** at a specific point in time: *Then one hot day....*

Sentence structure

In the second stanza sentences are quite short, particularly the one highlighted: *I sickened, turned, and ran*. Short sentences are used to build up dramatic tension and suspense. This sentence comes as the threats have built to a peak and the young boy decides to run away. It is broken into even shorter units by the use of commas, giving a moment's pause for thought before each action. This use of short sentences is in contrast to the rambling thirty-four word sentence in the first stanza. To best understand the effect of the sentence that begins *Here, every spring* you should re-read it out loud.

You should be feeling slightly out of breath by now! As you read that section of the poem you find yourself speeding up to fit all the words in before you run out of breath. This is intended to reflect the excitement and anticipation of **watching and waiting** for the hatching of the frogspawn. It also mirrors the final burst into life described at the end of the sentence. The technique of **enjambment** keeps the poem moving forward rather than breaking up the action with unnecessary commas and full stops.

Progress Check

1 How many syllables are there in the final line of the first stanza? (*For they were yellow in the sun and brown in rain.*)
2 How does the poet compensate for this in the next line?
3 What effect does this slight change to the rhythm have?

1 12   2 The next line is shorter – eight syllables.   3 It makes the short line more dramatic and links the two stanzas together.

3.4 Pre-1914 poetry – William Blake

William Blake wrote two books of poetry between 1785 and 1795 called *Songs of Innocence* and *Songs of Experience*. He was very concerned about social issues of the time, such as chimney sweep boys, the poor and the power of the church. He used his poetry to express his concerns to the public. The *Songs of Innocence* show the world how it could or should be, and the *Songs of Experience* show what Blake thought the world was really like.

Language differences

You may find that writing from another historical period is difficult to understand at first. **Sentence structure and word order** may be more complicated and some words may seem unfamiliar. However, with concentration and perseverance you should be able to overcome these difficulties.

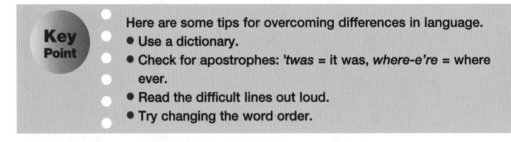

Key Point

Here are some tips for overcoming differences in language.
- Use a dictionary.
- Check for apostrophes: *'twas* = it was, *where-e're* = where ever.
- Read the difficult lines out loud.
- Try changing the word order.

Reading the poems

Key Point

Remember to read the poems three times, looking for different clues each time.

The two poems called 'Holy Thursday' were a complaint about the way orphan children were treated. As you read the poems, look for the differences in the way the people in the poems are presented.

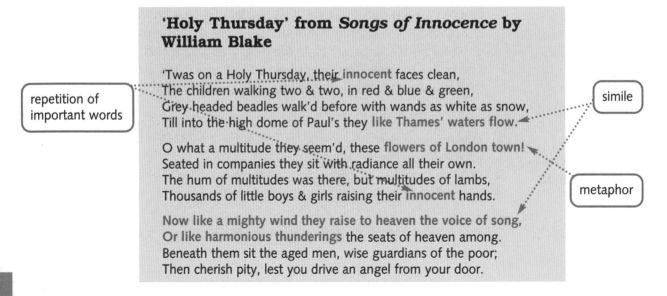

'Holy Thursday' from *Songs of Innocence* by William Blake

'Twas on a Holy Thursday, their innocent faces clean,
The children walking two & two, in red & blue & green,
Grey-headed beadles walk'd before with wands as white as snow,
Till into the high dome of Paul's they like Thames' waters flow.

O what a multitude they seem'd, these flowers of London town!
Seated in companies they sit with radiance all their own.
The hum of multitudes was there, but multitudes of lambs,
Thousands of little boys & girls raising their innocent hands.

Now like a mighty wind they raise to heaven the voice of song,
Or like harmonious thunderings the seats of heaven among.
Beneath them sit the aged men, wise guardians of the poor;
Then cherish pity, lest you drive an angel from your door.

repetition of important words

simile

metaphor

'Holy Thursday' from *Songs of Experience* by William Blake

Is this a holy thing to see,
In a rich and fruitful land,
Babes reduc'd to misery,
Fed with cold and usurous hand?

Is that trembling cry a song?
Can it be a song of joy?
And so many children poor?
It is a land of poverty!

And their sun does never shine,
And their fields are bleak & bare,
And their ways are fill'd with thorns;
It is eternal winter there.

For where-e'er the sun does shine,
And where-e'er the rain does fall,
Babe can never hunger there,
Nor poverty the mind appall.

Comparing the poems

You should be able to:
● trace the development of themes, ideas and values in texts.

The **first poem** is about the charity school children singing in St Paul's cathedral and giving thanks for the way they are looked after by the church elders. In this poem, the children are described in a positive way.

In the **second poem**, all the images and ideas are negative. Blake suggests that the first poem isn't really a true picture of the way the children are treated.

Vocabulary

● Innocence – in the first poem, the word *innocent* is used twice. This suggests that the children are harmless, that they need to be looked after and that anybody would be happy to take care of them.
● Lambs – in the first poem, the children are described as *lambs*, which links to the idea of innocence. The children are harmless and defenceless and the *wise guardians of the poor* look after them.
● *Poverty* – in the second poem, the word *poverty* is repeated. This suggests that the children have to go without comforts.
● *Bleak and bare* – in the second poem Blake creates the impression that everything is empty, cold and depressing. This contrasts with the bright colours of the first poem.

Imagery

Blake uses a range of images in the first poem:

● *The flowers of London town*

This **metaphor** is effective because it makes the children seem bright, cheerful and beautiful. People like to see flowers brightening up a town or city, and this image suggests that people like to see the children walking through the streets.

● *Like Thames' waters flow*

This **simile** is effective for many reasons:

- the Thames is important to the life of the city and this makes the children seem important to the city
- if you looked at the children from above, they might look like a river moving smoothly though the streets
- this image gives you a good idea of how many children there are.

● Their songs are described as *like a mighty wind* and *harmonious thunderings*.

- Using **similes** connected to the weather links the children to the innocence of nature.
- Thunder and wind are both powerful forces, and using these images gives the impression that the children's singing is also very powerful.

Use of imagery is limited in the **second poem** because Blake wants to be more direct and straightforward in his comments about the situation the charity school children are in. Their songs are now described as a *trembling cry*.

In the third stanza Blake creates the image of their lives lived out in the *eternal winter*. The sun never shines, the trees and fields are bare. Their journey through life is made difficult by thorny obstacles.

The adults in the poems

The way the children are presented is linked to the way Blake sees the people who are supposed to look after the children. In the **first poem** the descriptions are positive:

● *Grey-headed beadles walk'd before with wands as white as snow*.

- They are presented as the leaders, making sure the children go the right way.
- The description is quite neutral, so they seem harmless themselves.
- The simile *wands as white as snow* makes the reader think of innocence and purity.

● *Wise guardians of the poor*

- In this description, the word *wise* suggests that they will always do the right thing.
- A *guardian* looks after and protects somebody or something.

In the **second poem** the description of the men who 'look after' the children is negative:

● *Fed by cold usurous hand*. This description is effective for a number of reasons:

- there isn't an actual person mentioned in this poem, which suggests that the children are the responsibility of a faceless organisation
- the word *cold* suggests a lack of care or concern
- usury is the practice of lending money at unfairly high interest rates. In this poem the use of the word *usurous* suggests meanness and

greed. It also hints that money that should be used to help the children is being spent elsewhere.

Structure

Pre-1914 poetry tends to have **more formal structure** than later poetry.
- The **first poem** has three four-line stanzas. It is written in **rhyming couplets** and this makes the poem seem quite light-hearted and complete.
- The **second poem** is also written in four-line stanzas. However, the rhyme scheme is different. Although some of the lines rhyme and there is some patterning, **the rhyme is inconsistent** – this suits the tone of the poem.

Progress Check

1 There are lots of questions in the second poem. Why do you think this is?
2 How would we express *the seats of heaven among*?
3 What does *lest* mean?

1 It shows that he questions what happens to the children. **2** amongst the seats of heaven **3** in order not to

3.5 Comparing poems on a theme or subject

War poetry

You should be able to:
- **compare** the themes and style of at least two poets.

During the First World War, lots of soldiers wrote poetry in the trenches to record their feelings and fears. Much of this poetry is now recognised as some of the most powerful writing of the twentieth century.

Realism or patriotism?

Not all of the poets writing at this time had the same feelings about the war. The poetry written at this time falls into two broad categories:
- **realist** – the poets who wanted to represent the horror and grim reality of war
- **patriotic** – the poets who saw the war as a 'necessary evil' and who felt it was honourable and noble to be involved, and to die for your country if necessary.

Each of the following poems (on pages 50 and 51) represents one of these categories. As you read them, think about the **message** that each poet wants to deliver and how he tries to do this.

'Dulce Et Decorum Est'
by Wilfred Owen

Bent double, like old beggars under sacks,
Knock-kneed, coughing like hags, we cursed through sludge,
Till on the haunting flares we turned our backs
And towards our distant rest began to trudge.
Men marched asleep. Many had lost their boots
But limped on, blood-shod. All went lame; all blind;

Drunk with fatigue; deaf even to the hoots
Of gas shells dropping softly behind.
GAS! GAS! quick, boys! – An ecstasy of fumbling,
Fitting the clumsy helmets just in time;
But someone still was yelling out and stumbling,
And flound'ring like a man in fire or lime...
Dim, through the misty panes and thick green light,
As under a green sea, I saw him drowning.

In all my dreams, before my helpless sight,
He plunges at me, guttering, choking, drowning.

If in some smothering dreams you too could pace
Behind the wagon that we flung him in,
And watch the white eyes writhing in his face,
His hanging face, like a devil's sick of sin;
If you could hear, at every jolt, the blood
Come gargling from the froth-corrupted lungs,
Obscene as cancer, bitter as the cud
Of vile, incurable sores on innocent tongues, –
My friend, you would not tell with such high zest
To children ardent for some desperate glory,
The old Lie: *Dulce et decorum est*
Pro patria mori.

'The Soldier' *by Rupert Brooke*

If I should die, think only this of me:
That there's some corner of a foreign field
That is forever England. There shall be
In that rich earth a richer dust concealed;
A dust whom England bore, shaped, made aware,
Gave, once, her flowers to love, her ways to roam,
A body of England's, breathing English air,
Washed by rivers, blest by suns of home.

And think, this heart, all evil shed away,
A pulse in the eternal mind, no less
Gives somewhere back the thoughts by England given;
Her sights and sounds; dreams happy as her day;
And laughter, learnt of friends; and gentleness,
In hearts at peace, under English heaven.

Comparing the poems

Title

The title of the **first poem** is not immediately easy to understand. It links to the final lines of the poem, which declare that the sentiment expressed in this Latin phrase is a lie. The title is **ironic** because the whole poem sets out to prove that it isn't sweet and honourable to die for your country in this way.

The title of the **second poem**, 'The Soldier', is far more **straightforward**. In the poem this soldier expresses his thoughts about dying for his country.

Tone/attitude

Wilfred Owen was a **realist**. He clearly describes the **horror** of war in his poem and doesn't shy away from the terrible things that he has seen. He is keen that people at home should know exactly how terrible and frightening it is to be involved in the fighting.

Rupert Brooke was far more **patriotic** and more likely to agree with the Latin phrase in Owen's poem. Although the soldier doesn't claim to enjoy the war, he does seem proud to fight for his country. His message is that dying for England is a worthwhile reason for dying. He makes the idea of death seem quite **romantic and painless**.

Vocabulary

Wilfred Owen's poem contains lots of negative vocabulary:
- illness/disease – *coughing, vile sores, cancer, lame, blind*
- tiredness – *distant rest, fatigue, asleep*
- inability to breathe – *drowning, choking, guttering, smothering.*

Rupert Brooke's poem is far more positive:

- the words *England* or *English* are repeated six times
- positive emotions and concepts – **love, laughter, friendship, gentleness, peace, happiness**.

Both poets mention dreams. Owen's are *smothering dreams*, full of the real horrors he has seen during the war. Brooke's soldier refers to *dreams happy as her day*.

Voice

Both poems are written in the **first person**. Owen's poem is written in his own voice, speaking from bitter personal experience. This makes the terrible events he writes about seem very direct and real. Brooke's poem is written in the persona of a brave and proud soldier who feels he owes his life to his country.

Imagery

There are many **effective images** in **Wilfred Owen's** poem. All of the images in the poem have been highlighted in the text. Read the poem again and try to explain why each image is effective. The first one has been done for you.

Owen uses two similes to show how tired and ill the soldiers are:
> Bent double, like old beggars under sacks,
> Knock-kneed, coughing like hags, we cursed through sludge,

These images are very direct and unpleasant and immediately show that Owen does not believe the sentiment expressed in the title of his poem. During the war, people wanted to imagine brave, healthy soldiers fighting for their country. Owen shows that, although they may have joined the army in that state, the war has damaged them beyond repair.

Brooke's poem is simpler and less densely packed with imagery. However, he does use **personification** to represent England as a woman.

A dust whom England bore...
Gave, once, <u>her</u> flowers to love...

Why do you think Brooke used this form of imagery?

Structure

The **first poem** has a regular **rhythm and rhyme** scheme. It keeps the poem moving forward. It is divided into four stanzas. The third stanza is only two lines in length, which makes it stand out and gives the lines more impact. This is effective because in these lines Owen explains how he is constantly haunted by the image of another soldier's death.

The punctuation and sentence structure in the poem are used to create a variety of effects.

GAS! GAS! Quick, boys! – An ecstasy of fumbling

The exclamation marks show strong feeling – in this case, terror. They also help to recreate the reality and urgency of somebody shouting.

The **second poem** is written following many of the conventions of a **sonnet**. It is fourteen lines long with ten syllables in each line.

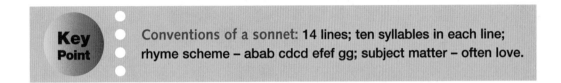

The English sonnet is a **traditional** form made popular by William Shakespeare. The values in this poem are also very traditional, so it makes sense to use the sonnet form.

The sonnet is most often connected to the theme of **love**. Although this poem is about war, one of the central themes is the love of and willingness to die for England.

> **Key Point**
>
> **Conventions of a sonnet: 14 lines; ten syllables in each line; rhyme scheme – abab cdcd efef gg; subject matter – often love.**

Your response

Although it is possible to learn how to identify images and structural features, there is no substitute for a **personal response** to poetry.

- How do these poems make you **feel**?
- Which one did you **prefer**?
- Which poem was easiest to **connect** with?
- What do you think particular **images mean**?

Progress Check

1 What emotion does Owen feel towards the person he addresses as *my friend* in the poem?
2 Who are the *children ardent for some desperate glory*?
3 What is the rhyme scheme of 'The Soldier'?

1 anger **2** Young boys waiting to sign up to join the war. **3** abab cdcd efgefg

Practice test questions

The following questions will help you to prepare for the Optional Tests in Years 7 and 8.

Read the poem below.

'Hide and Seek' *by Vernon Scannell*

Yoohoo! I'm ready! Come and find me!
The sacks in the toolshed smell like the seaside.
You make yourself little in the salty dark,
Close your eyes tight and hope your feet aren't showing.
Better not risk another call, they might be close.   **5**
Don't sneeze whatever happens. The floor is cold.
They're probably searching the bushes near the swing.
What's that? That sounds like them. They're coming in!
Don't breathe or move. Still. Someone knocks a can.
Feet mutter. Somebody comes very close,   **10**
A scuffle of words, a laugh, and then they're gone.
They might be back. Careful in case they come.
They'll try the greenhouse, then in here again.
They're taking a long time, but they'll come back.
Risk a peep out, perhaps? Not yet; they might creep in.   **15**
A good hiding-place, this: the best you've ever found.
It's funny though, they haven't tried again.
Can't hear a thing. They must be miles away.
The dark damp smell of sand is thicker now.
Give them another call: *Yoo-hoo! Come and find me!*   **20**
But they are still elsewhere. They'll think you're clever,
And ask you where you hid. Don't tell them. Keep it secret.
It's cold in here. You can't hear anything.
But wait. Let them hunt a little longer;
Think of them frowning at each other   **25**
Where can he be? We've looked all over.
Something tickles on your nose. Your legs are stiff.
Just a little longer and then creep out.
They're not coming back. You've tricked them properly.
All right. Push off the sacks. That's better.   **30**
Good to be rid of that unpleasant smell.
Out of the shed. *Hey! Here I am! I'm here!*
I've won the game! You couldn't find me!
The darkening garden watches. Nothing stirs.
The bushes hold their breath. The air is cold.   **35**
Yes, here you are, but where are they who sought you?

---

1 Explain what happens in this poem.   **[2]**

2 Read lines 29–36 again and think about what happens earlier in the poem.
How does the boy feel about being alone?   **[1]**

3 Comment on the effectiveness of the punctuation in lines 8–10.   **[2]**

4 What is different about the lines in italics?   **[1]**

The following question will help you prepare for SATs in Year 9.

Assessment: AT2

'Blackberry Picking' *by Seamus Heaney*

Late August, given heavy rain and sun
For a full week, the blackberries would ripen.
At first, just one, a glossy purple clot
Among others, red, green, hard as a knot.
You ate the first one and its flesh was sweet
Like thickened wine: summer's blood was in it
Leaving stains upon the tongue and lust for
Picking. Then red ones inked up and that hunger
Sent us out with milk-cans, pea-tins, jam-pots
Where briars scratched and wet grass bleached our boots.
Round hayfields, cornfields and potato-drills
We trekked and picked until the cans were full,
Until the tinkling bottom had been covered
With green ones, and on top big dark blobs burned
Like a plate of eyes. Our hands were peppered
With thorn pricks, our palms sticky as Bluebeard's.

We hoarded the fresh berries in the byre.
But when the bath was filled we found a fur,
A rat grey fungus, glutting on our cache.
The juice was stinking too. Once off the bush
The fruit fermented, the sweet flesh would turn sour.
I always felt like crying. It wasn't fair
That all the lovely canfuls smelt of rot.
Each year I hoped they would keep, knew they would not.

Glossary

Bluebeard: a pirate who killed many of his wives by chopping off their heads

byre: a cowshed

cache: a hidden store of treasure, provisions or weapons

How does the poet recreate his memories of childhood in this poem?

Think about:
● the way actions are described
● the structure, imagery and vocabulary used in the poem.

Marks: 6

4 Reading non-fiction

To achieve the following National Curriculum levels you need to

Level 4
- find information and ideas in a text
- explain your views of a text
- be aware of the purpose of the text

Level 5
- identify key features, themes and characters in a text
- select sentences, phrases and relevant information to support your views
- collect and collate information from different sources

Level 6
- identify different layers of meaning
- comment on the significance and effect of different devices, including layout where appropriate
- summarise a range of information from different sources

Level 7
- show understanding of the way information is conveyed in a range of texts
- select and analyse information and ideas
- give a personal response to the text

4.1 Reading autobiography

Literary non-fiction

Writers of autobiography, biography and travel writing use many of the same devices and techniques as fiction writers because, although these texts are based on fact, the main purpose is to entertain.

Recount

Autobiography follows the main conventions of this non-fiction style: events are retold in chronological order; it is written in the past tense using time connectives; it focuses on identified groups of people.

An autobiography is a personal life story. The author selects and reconstructs events from their own life to share with the public. A personal account may be biased, and may leave out some details whilst emphasising others for effect. The following extract from Laurie Lee's autobiography, *Cider with Rosie*, recounts one of his earliest memories. As you read it, think about the techniques he uses to bring his account to life.

Key Point

Bias – if a piece of writing is biased, it takes a particular point of view; unbiased writing is balanced and takes account of both sides of an argument.

emotive language

extended metaphor

repetition

simile

simile

simile

I was set down from the carrier's cart at the age of three; and there with a sense of **bewilderment and terror** my life in the village began.

The June grass, amongst which I stood, was taller than I was, and I wept. I had never been so close to grass before. It **towered** above me and all around me, each blade tattooed with tiger-skins of sunlight. It was knife-edged, **dark and a wicked** green, **thick as a forest** and alive with grasshoppers that chirped and chattered and **leapt through the air like monkeys**.

I was lost and didn't know where to move. A tropic heat oozed up from the ground, rank with sharp odours of roots and nettles. **Snow-clouds** of elder-blossom banked in the sky, **showering** upon me the fumes and **flakes** of their sweet and giddy suffocation. High overhead ran **frenzied** larks, **screaming, as though the sky were tearing apart.**

For the first time in my life I was out of the sight of humans. For **the first time in my life** I was alone in a world whose behaviour I could neither predict nor fathom: a world of birds that squealed, of plants that stank, of insects that sprang about without warning. I was lost and I did not expect to be found again. I put back my head and howled, and the sun hit me smartly on the face, **like a bully.**

From this daylight nightmare I was wakened, as from many another, by the appearance of my sisters. They came scrambling and calling up the steep rough bank, and parting the long grass found me. Faces of rose, familiar, living; huge shining faces **hung up like shields** between me and the sky; faces with grins and white teeth (some broken) to be **conjured up like genii** with a howl, brushing off terror with their broad scoldings and affection. They leaned over me – one, two, three – their mouths smeared with red currants and their hands dripping with juice.

"There, there, it's all right, don't you wail any more. Come down 'ome and we'll stuff you with currants."

From *Cider With Rosie* by Laurie Lee

Word level

Autobiography is from the Greek words: **autos** – self, **bios** – life and **graphein** – to write. An autobiography is a 'self-written life story'.

To learn the spelling of this word, split it into the three parts and learn to spell each section: **Auto bio graphy**. This method will help you to learn lots of other words too, such as **autograph, biology, photograph**.

Progress Check

1 Which two words in the first sentence show how the boy feels?
2 Why is the boy frightened?
3 How many sentences in the second paragraph are complex sentences?
4 Which phrase is repeated to show that the boy is experiencing something unfamiliar?
5 Find an example of a simile used to describe his sisters.

1 *bewilderment and terror* 2 *He can't see any people and is lost.* 3 *three* 4 *For the first time in my life…* 5 *like shields…, like genii…*

Understanding an autobiography text

You should be able to:

- comment on how writers convey setting, character and mood through word choice and sentence structure
- recognise how writers' language choices can enhance meaning.

To show your understanding of the way an author writes and the choices he or she makes, you should be able to write about a range of features in the text.

Setting and mood

The way the setting is described helps to convey the **mood** of this piece of writing. Laurie Lee is writing about the first time he saw a place and he found the experience very frightening. The language he uses emphasises his fear.

Key Point

Setting – where the action takes place.
Mood – the way a piece of writing makes you feel or the way the characters in the text feel.

Emotive vocabulary

- In the first sentence, the words *bewilderment* and *terror* are used to set a mood of fear and confusion.
- The word *towered*, used to describe the tall grass, is a powerful word that makes the grass seem threatening. He also describes the grass as being *a wicked green*.
- He uses the words *frenzied* and *screaming* to describe the larks. This makes the situation sound dangerous. If he wanted to create a happy mood he might have used the words *excited* and *singing*.
- The phrase a *tropic heat oozed* makes you think of a jungle or a rain forest.

Figurative language

Similes

The author uses this device to make an English meadow seem like a dangerous and unfamiliar jungle. An adult reader might not be able to imagine being frightened in a field, but the similes help to create an unfamiliar setting – being lost in a jungle would frighten most people! The grass is described as being *as thick as a forest* and the grasshoppers are *like monkeys*.

The author also uses similes to change familiar symbols. The sun is usually connected with pleasant feelings. However, because he is so frightened even the sun becomes dangerous: *the sun hit me smartly on the face, like a bully.*

Metaphors

The grass is described as being *tattooed with tiger skins of sunlight*. This image links to the jungle idea, but it also gives the reader a sense of how close the grass was because the description is so detailed.

This is an extended metaphor.

The elder blossom is described in terms of the weather. The author uses the words *snow-clouds*, *showering* and *flakes* to describe the flowers. He uses this description because the blossom is white and it is blown across the sky in clouds. It also adds to the confusion he feels – it is a hot, summer day but he uses the imagery of winter.

Characters

In the final paragraphs the author introduces his sisters, and this changes the mood of the text.

Description

Things have been described as unfamiliar, but his sisters are safe and familiar; they are very real: *white teeth (some broken)*; *broad scoldings and affection*; *their mouths smeared with red currants.*

Their voices are brought to life with the representation of their accent and dialect: *"come down 'ome and we'll stuff you with currants."*

Sentence structure

Throughout this extract there is a variety of sentence structures. This makes the writing more interesting and lively.

In the fourth paragraph, the opening two sentences begin in exactly the same way: *For the first time in my life*. This repetition emphasises the fact that he faces an unfamiliar situation.

> **Key Point**
>
> Sentence structure – **this is the way sentences are put together. See Chaptert 11 for simple, compound and complex sentences.**

The second sentence is a **complex sentence**, which contrasts with the **simple sentences** surrounding it.

After the colon in the complex sentence there is a list of the dangers he faces (notice the use of commas). The **punctuation** within the sentence helps to create a sense of the problems mounting up.

The sentence that follows is a compound sentence, giving equal weight to both clauses. This allows the author to make his opinion sound like a statement of fact, making it more powerful: *I was lost and did not expect to be found again*.

Word level

Genii is the plural form of **genie**. Other words that form their plural in this way end in **-us** and have Latin roots.

Rule: to form the plural replace the **-us** with **-i**.

Examples: cactus → cacti   radius → radii

Have a go: What are the plurals of **fungus**, **locus** and **genius**?

Progress Check

1 The cues to start a new paragraph are: **time**, **topic** or **talk**. What is the most common reason for a change of paragraph in the extract from *Cider with Rosie*? TIME/TOPIC/TALK

2 Is the particular way you pronounce words known as your **accent** or your **dialect**?

3 A compound sentence has more than one clause. TRUE or FALSE?

4 A simile is a comparison of two objects using the words *like* or *as*. TRUE or FALSE?

5 A topic sentence appears at the **beginning/middle/end** of a paragraph.

1 topic   2 accent   3 true   4 true   5 beginning

4.2 Reading travel writing

What is travel writing?

Travel writing is another form of **recount** and is very similar to **autobiography**. You need to look out for the same features and textual conventions when reading travel writing as you do when reading autobiography.

In travel writing, places and the people who live there are emphasized.

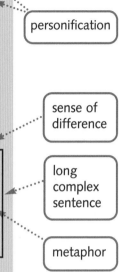

Read the following extract and think about what kind of impression you are given about the place that is described and the people who live there.

rhetorical question

emotive vocabulary

verb choices

emotive vocabulary

personification

sense of difference

long complex sentence

metaphor

And so I went to Edinburgh. **Can there anywhere be a more beautiful and beguiling city to arrive at by train early on a crisp, dark Novembery evening?** To emerge from the bustling, **subterranean bowels** of Waverley Station and find yourself in the very **heart** of such a glorious city is a happy experience indeed. I hadn't been to Edinburgh for years and had forgotten just how **captivating** it can be. Every monument was lit with golden floodlights – the castle and Bank of Scotland headquarters on the hill, the Balmoral Hotel and the Scott Memorial down below – which gave them a certain **eerie grandeur**. The city was abustle with end-of-day activity. Buses **swept** through Princes Street and shop and office workers **scurried** along the pavements, **hastening** home to have their haggis and **cock-a-leekie** soup and indulge in a few **skirls** or whatever it is Scots do when the sun goes **doon**.

I'd booked a room in the Caledonian Hotel, which was a rash and **extravagant** thing to do, but it's a **terrific** building and an Edinburgh institution and I just had to be part of it for one night, so I set off for it down Princes Street, past the **Gothic rocket ship** of the Scott Memorial, unexpectedly **exhilarated** to find myself among the hurrying throngs and the sight of the castle on its craggy mount outlined against a pale evening sky.

From *Notes from a Small Island* by Bill Bryson

Key Point

● Rhetorical question – a question that does not require an answer. Rhetorical questions are used for emphasis or to create particular effects.

Word level

Doon – Scottish pronunciation of the word **down**.

Skirl – the shrill sound made by bagpipes.

Bill Bryson includes these words to give a sense of the place he is writing about.

Understanding of a piece of travel writing

People

The **people** are not described in any detail in this passage. The writer creates the impression that they are busy, a little distant and different to people he has encountered in other parts of Britain.

Place

The writer creates a **romantic picture** of a beautiful but very busy city. He gives the impression that, like the people who live there, Edinburgh is somehow alien and different to other places he has visited.

Vocabulary choices

- **Emotive vocabulary** – the writer uses words like *beautiful*, *beguiling* and *captivating* to suggest that he has fallen in love with the city. The phrase *eerie grandeur* makes the city seem imposing and slightly frightening.
- **Verb choices** – the writer chooses the verbs *swept*, *scurried*, *hastening* and *hurrying* to describe the movement of people and objects in Edinburgh. This gives the impression that everybody is busy and things move very quickly. It makes the place seem lively.

Figurative language and language devices

- **Alliteration** – in the opening sentences of the passage the writer creates patterns by using alliteration – *beautiful and beguiling city... the bustling subterranean bowels of Waverley Station*. The description of the city is quite poetic and romantic; the use of alliteration enhances this.
- **Personification** – if Edinburgh is a person, then the underground station represents the *bowels* of the city. The station is dark and dirty; it provides a strong contrast with the beautiful city above the ground. The writer continues the image by referring to the *heart* of the city.
- **Metaphor** – by describing the monument as a *gothic rocket ship*, the writer gives the impression that it has landed there from another planet. This adds to the atmosphere of difference that he has created throughout this passage.

Sentence structure

The opening sentence is a **simple sentence**: a statement of fact, which introduces the topic of the whole passage. The rest of the passage is mostly written in extended **complex** and **compound sentences**.

The second sentence is a **rhetorical question**; it makes the reader more involved and requires them to imagine the place that is being described.

The final sentence is very long. Each **clause** in the sentence is used to build up a sense of excitement and wonderment as the writer explores the city. This sentence also reflects the description of the **hurrying throng**.

Below is another extract from Bill Bryson's book.

I took a train to Liverpool. They were having a festival of litter when I arrived. Citizens had taken time off from their busy activities to add crisp packets, empty cigarette boxes, and carrier-bags to the otherwise bland and neglected landscape. They fluttered gaily in the bushes and brought colour and texture to pavements and gutters. And to think that elsewhere we stick these objects in rubbish bags.

In another bout of extravagant madness, I had booked a room in the Adelphi Hotel. I had seen it from the street on earlier visits and it appeared to have an old-fashioned grandeur about it that I was keen to investigate. On the other hand, it looked expensive and I wasn't sure my trousers could stand another session in the trouser press. So I was most agreeably surprised when I checked in to discover that I was entitled to a special weekend rate and that there would be money spare for a nice meal and a

parade of beer in any of the many wonderful pubs in which Liverpool specializes.

And so, soon afterwards, I found myself, like all fresh arrivals in Liverpool, in the grand and splendorous surroundings of the Philharmonic, clutching a pint glass...

From *Notes from a Small Island* by Bill Bryson

Progress Check

Answer the following questions about the passage above.

1 What kind of sentence is the first sentence in the passage?
simple/complex/compound
2 What is the name of the device used in the phrase *splendorous surroundings*?
3 Does the opening description of Liverpool create a positive or negative impression?
4 Does the writer like Liverpool?

1 simple 2 alliteration 3 negative 4 yes

4.3 Reading leaflets

Text conventions of leaflets

YORKSHIRE MUSEUM, MUSEUM GARDENS, YORK

The Upright Ape

colourful pictures

MEET YOUR ANCESTORS!
20 July to 16 February
at the
Yorkshire Museum, Museum Gardens, York   YORK

exclamation

Leaflets follow a range of non-fiction conventions.

- **Information text** – leaflets follow many of the conventions of this non-fiction text style: **purpose**: to give information; **structure**: clearly organised; **language**: present tense, third person.
- **Persuasive text** – leaflets are often intended to persuade as well as inform. The conventions of persuasive texts are: **structure**: statement of argument followed by a range of persuasive points in favour of the argument; **language**: present tense, often in the second person, emotive and persuasive language.
- **Layout** – what a leaflet looks like is very important. Features of layout include: pictures, columns, font size and style.

Look at this leaflet, which is continued on page 64, to see how effective these conventions are.

persuasive panel

imperative verb

MEET YOUR ANCESTORS!

Who are we?

Where do we come from?

Find the answers to these questions in our new exhibition 'The Upright Ape'.

Discover your roots with the aid of exciting hands-on displays, stunning life size reconstructions and real fossils.

Walk in the footsteps of an ape, keep watch for deadly leopards and test your strength against a Neanderthal – a truly interactive experience awaits you.

The Upright Ape is a hands-on journey through time which will entertain and intrigue all age groups.

directive

Other exhibitions and events this year

Alcuin and Charlemagne – The Golden Age of York
The story is told through the letters of Alcuin, richly illuminated books, sculptures and precious objects of ivory, crystal, silver and gold.
Until 26 September

W A Ismay Collection
A celebration of the lifelong passion of Bill Ismay, whose spectacular collection of post-war studio pottery was recently bequeathed to the Yorkshire Museum.
From 8 September

Wildlife Photographer of the Year Exhibition
See the winning and highly commended entries from this worldwide competition.
17 November to 26 January

I would like to receive information on events and new exhibitions at the Yorkshire Museum, York Castle Museum and York City Art Gallery.

Name_____

Address_____
_____

Postcode_____

e-mail address_____

I would prefer to receive information by:
e-mail ☐   Post ☐

To be included on the mailing list please return this completed form to: Marketing Department, Yorkshire Museum, Museum Gardens, York, YO1 7FR.

information panel

lots of pictures

written in 2nd person to involve the reader

YORKSHIRE MUSEUM
MUSEUM GARDENS, YORK

Set in 10 acres of botanical gardens in the centre of York, the Yorkshire Museum houses some of the richest archaeological finds in Europe and covers over 1000 years of local history.

Take a journey back through time and discover the Roman, Anglo-Saxon, Viking and Medieval history and treasures of York and Yorkshire. Don't miss the exquisite world-famous Middleham Jewel, a 15th century gold pendant adorned with a magnificent sapphire.

You can also visit the Abbey Gallery and the majestic ruin of the medieval St Mary's Abbey, once one of the most wealthy and powerful abbeys in the north.

Also, meet the Jurassic sea dragons in the Hunters and Hunted Gallery.

persuasive panel

directive

YORKSHIRE MUSEUM, MUSEUM GARDENS, YORK

OPEN DAILY 10am – 5pm

The Yorkshire Museum is situated in the Museum Gardens in the centre of York, just a short walk from York Railway Station. Follow the signs to the city centre. There is a regular Park and Ride service from four sites on main routes as you enter York and there are also two car parks within a short walk of the museum.

ADMISSION
Adults £4.50
Child/Concession £2.95
Family £14.00 (2 adults and up to 3 children)

Group bookings and school parties welcome. Call for details of group rates.

York residents are entitled to free entry to the Yorkshire Museum permanent collections and reduced entry to touring exhibitions, on presentation of a YorkCard.

5 DAY MUSEUM PASS
allowing unlimited entry into Yorkshire Museum, York Castle Museum and York City Art Gallery.
Adult £9.00   Child/Concession £5.00   Family £27.50

All galleries are accessible to wheelchair users and toilet facilities are available to all visitors.
The museum shop has an extensive range of gifts to remind you of your visit.

For further information please contact:

Yorkshire Museum   Tel: (01904) 551800
Museum Gardens   Fax: (01904) 551802
York   e-mail: yorkshire.museum@york.gov.uk
YO1 7FR   www.york.gov.uk

information panel

map

YORK
MARYGATE
YORK CITY ART GALLERY
YORKSHIRE MUSEUM
MUSEUM GARDENS
RAILWAY STATION
York Minster
RIVER OUSE
LENDAL BRIDGE
ROUGIER STREET
LENDAL

HOW TO FIND US

Sentence types

Statements

A **statement** is a sentence that gives information to the reader. This kind of sentence ends with a full stop. These sentences are used in the information sections of the leaflet – in the *Other exhibitions and events...* and *OPEN DAILY* panels of the leaflet.

The Yorkshire Museum is situated...

All galleries are accessible to wheelchair users...

Exclamations

An **exclamation** is usually a short sentence that shows strong feelings.

In this leaflet the exclamation *Meet your ancestors!* is used twice. In this case the exclamation mark indicates surprise. It is linked to the pictures of the 'upright apes' and suggests that human beings are directly related to the apes.

Directives

A **directive** is a sentence that expects someone to do something. If it is a sharp command, the sentence should end with an **exclamation mark** – Shut up! Sit down!

This leaflet contains polite instructions that aim to persuade.

Discover your roots with the aid of exciting hands-on displays...

Walk in the footsteps of an ape...

Commands or instructions use the **imperative** form of the verb – *discover*, *walk*, *find*.

Questions

A **question** is a sentence that asks for information and requires an answer.

In this leaflet the questions are concerned with human origins. They are the kind of 'big questions' that people ask themselves when they are thinking about how they fit into life.

Who are we? Where do we come from?

The leaflet claims that the exhibition has all the answers to these questions.

Progress Check

1 How many exclamations are there in the leaflet?
2 How much does a family museum pass cost?
3 What form of verb is used in this sentence: *Also, meet the Jurassic sea dragons...* ?
4 What is the main exhibition called?

1 two **2** £27.50 **3** imperative **4** The Upright Ape

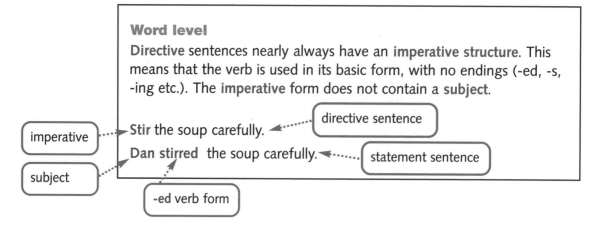

Word level

Directive sentences nearly always have an **imperative structure**. This means that the verb is used in its basic form, with no endings (-ed, -s, -ing etc.). The **imperative** form does not contain a **subject**.

imperative ·····► Stir the soup carefully. ◄······ directive sentence

Dan stirred the soup carefully. ◄······· statement sentence

subject ·····►

-ed verb form

Vocabulary choices

This leaflet uses lots of **persuasive** vocabulary, particularly in the inside section: *exciting, stunning, deadly, entertain and intrigue*.

This kind of language makes the display sound appealing and worth visiting.

The information sections also contain persuasive language – *richly illuminated books*.

Layout

- **Pictures** – the pictures are colourful and take up a large proportion of the page. They are intended to show that the apes look similar to human beings.

- **Colour** – the leaflet is very colourful and appealing. The writing is white so that it stands out clearly from the background.

- **Titles** – the titles are larger than the rest of the text. *The Upright Ape* title is in a different font style because it is the main title.

- **Columns and paragraphs** – the text is in columns and short paragraphs, which make it easier to read. The columns make it easier to identify the informative and persuasive sections.

- **Other features** – information about prices and opening times is presented in note form.

  Admission
  Adults £4.50

To judge the **effectiveness** of this leaflet you should consider all of these points together. Do you think it would be effective in persuading people to visit the exhibition? Would you visit the exhibition after reading this leaflet?

> You should be able to:
> - analyse the overall structure of a text to identify how key ideas are developed.

Word level

Prepositions hold sentences together – they are the words that show how one thing is related to another: **to, between, off, on, into, above, beneath**.

Find the answers to these questions...

The story is told through the letters of Alcuin...

4.4 Reading advertisements

How an advertisement is put together

When you read an advertisement there are many factors you should consider, including:

- target audience
- brand names
- slogans
- pictures and colour
- special offers/coupons
- emotive/persuasive vocabulary.

Target audience

Advertisers aim particular products at different groups of people according to age, sex, social class and interests. They will often make assumptions about people and label or stereotype them.

Who do you think these products would be aimed at: nappies, diamonds, mint chocolates, sports cars?

What kind of products would be aimed at these people: teenagers, 25-year-old single men, 40-year-old working mums?

Brand names

Brand names are chosen carefully. They can suggest particular lifestyles, values or interests and are intended to appeal to the target audience.

Nissan Primera: this suggests quality. Primera is similar to premium and premier.

Ford Ka: the spelling of Ka suggests novelty and simplicity. It is modern and futuristic. It is also bound to stick in your mind when you are looking for a new car!

Slogans

A slogan has to be catchy and memorable. Slogans use a range of devices: alliteration, repetition, puns, questions, personal pronouns and humour.

Have a break. Have a Kit Kat.   Repetition

The totally tropical taste.   Alliteration

Pictures and colour

All pictures try to make you feel something and most are biased, even photographs. They create a view of what the world is like using different tricks such as lighting and colour.

Different colours have different associations that can be linked to particular products.

Yellow: freshness, sunlight, lemons. This colour would be good for advertising washing up liquid.

Green: countryside, natural, healthy. What would you use this colour for?

What do you associate these colours with: red, black, orange, gold, blue?

Special offers/coupons

Advertisers often appear to offer 'something for nothing': if you buy one product you will receive another one free or half price. These offers are an **incentive** to try a new product or to encourage **loyalty** to an existing one.

Emotive/persuasive vocabulary

In advertising you will find lots of words and phrases that are intended to persuade you or appeal to your emotions.

tempting	silky	free
chocolate	romantic	powerful
creamy	traditional	mouthwatering
luxurious	like mum used to make	

Progress Check

1 Who would these words and phrases appeal to: look younger, healthy, firmer, smooth, creamy?

2 What kind of device does this slogan use? *The future's bright. The future's Orange.*

3 What is a target audience?

1 Middle-aged women concerned about the appearance of their skin. **2** repetition **3** The group of people a product is aimed at.

Analysing an advertisement

In order to assess the effectiveness of an advertisement, you must consider the importance of each element of the factors discussed above.

Study the advert on page 69, and then read about how each element has been used.

● **Target audience** – this advert is aimed at people who have a lot of time and money – the cruise is 69 nights and costs nearly £8000. The style of the advert – lots of text, rich colours and continued reference to warmth – suggests that it is aimed at retired couples who like to travel.

● **Picture** – the colours are warm and relaxing and link to those mentioned in the text. The picture is appealing and inviting. It makes the location seem romantic.

● **Slogan** – *At home, the world over.* This slogan suggests home comforts and familiarity in an unfamiliar environment. The cruise is over two months long, so the ship will become the passengers' home.

● **Special offers** – the *25% off* offer is in bold type to attract attention. It is used to encourage people to book early, as it is only available for a limited time.

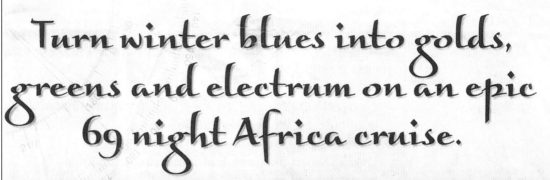

Turn winter blues into golds, greens and electrum on an epic 69 night Africa cruise.

Instead of enduring the January shivers, chill out in the sun
as you weave your way around the dark continent, leisurely unearthing its scenic splendour and historic legends.

Over two and a half months and 17,000 miles, Black Watch takes you on a truly relaxing voyage that you'll never forget.
From the Canaries to the biblical desert beauty of Namibia and the breathtaking vista of Cape Town's Table Mountain.

Next, into the Indian Ocean and ashore, at Richard's Bay, the chance of some wildlife spotting in one of KwaZulu-Natal's reserves.
Then on to Madagascar, Kenya, the Seychelles, the magnificent temples of the Nile, and fabled Petra in Jordan. In all, 26 unforgettable
ports of call, including the Greek islands and Tangier on the homeward leg. Departs Jan 5th. Prices from £7845*.

If 69 nights is too long to be away, don't worry. Our range of fly/cruises offer a shorter escape to the sun and additional land stays
are available, offering you the opportunity to go on extra excursions or time to shop and relax.
Departure dates are from early January to mid March.

Up to 25% off.

A dramatic voyage with substantial benefits. Book now and save up to 25%, with free travel insurance. On a 69 night cruise that would be
a considerable saving. Free coach transfers from 1200 points in the UK, or free standard class rail travel is also included.
Chase away those winter blues. Call Page & Moy now.

To book, call
0870 010 6444
quoting reference
CCP/RAD84R

Fred. Olsen Cruise Lines
AT HOME, THE WORLD OVER

PAGE &MOY LTD

www.fredolsen.co.uk

Conditions: 1. Valid on new phone bookings to Page & Moy. Each operator's booking conditions apply. 2. Discounts are refundable to Page & Moy on cancellation and based on tour operator's invoice basic cost.
fer is valid for bookings until "31st March 2001" unless otherwise stated. 4. All holidays are subject to availability. The list of tour operators and the example savings published are correct at time of going to press. 5. Comprehensive
rance cover is required at time of booking. 6. There will be a charge of £4.50 for all late bookings within 10 weeks of departure. 7. This offer cannot be combined with any other and existing bookings with tour operators or other
its cannot be transferred. 8. Page & Moy act as travel agent ABTA 99529 for tour operators who hold fully bonded ATOL licences. Cruise lines are members of the Passenger Shipping Association. 9. This offer is open to
f the UK, Channel Islands and the Isle of Man only, aged 18 years and over. *Prices are subject to availability and are based on 2 adults sharing an inside twin cabin and includes all meals, entertainment on board and port taxes.

You should be able to:
● recognise bias and objectivity, distinguishing facts from theories or opinions.

● **Emotive/persuasive vocabulary** – the main copy is full of emotive and persuasive vocabulary: *leisurely unearthing its scenic splendour and historic legends*.

The language is intended to make the reader feel relaxed and it emphasises the beauty, history and romantic nature of the cruise. The language is quite lyrical and poetic – *the biblical desert beauty of Namibia*. This also helps to emphasise the romance of discovery and adventure.

> **Word level**
>
> Articles are like **prepositions**: sentences don't make sense without them. An **article** is a **determiner** that introduces a **noun** or **noun phrase** (see **Chapter 11**).
>
> ● Definite article: **the**.
>   *Next, into <u>the</u> Indian Ocean* – there is only one Indian Ocean, so you must use the **definite** article
> ● Indefinite article: **a** or **an**.
>   (Use **an** when the noun that follows begins with a **vowel** – a, e, i, o, u.)
>   *<u>A</u> considerable saving. . . on <u>an</u> epic 69 night cruise. . .*

Progress Check

1 What kind of information does the small print contain?
2 *Departs Jan. 5th. Prices from £7845.* FACT or OPINION?
3 Is there more fact or more opinion in this advertisement?
4 Which season will the cruise help you to avoid?

1 terms and conditions 2 fact 3 opinion 4 winter

4.5 Reading newspapers

Key Point

Broadsheet – a newspaper considered to be more factual and serious in tone than a tabloid newspaper. Aims to inform rather than entertain. Examples: *The Guardian*, *The Times*.

Tabloid – aims to inform and entertain. A tabloid paper is more likely to use emotive language and sensationalise stories. Pictures and headlines are far more important in a tabloid. Examples: *The Sun*, *The Mirror*.

If you **compare** two newspaper articles from different newspaper formats, you will notice **differences** in many of the areas discussed below.

Analysing a newspaper story

When you are studying a newspaper report, you should think about the following.

● **Layout**
  ● How is the article broken up?
  ● Is the headline effective? How much of the page does it take up? Does it use any language devices?
  ● Where does the story appear in the newspaper?
  ● What use is made of pictures, captions and sub-headings?

● **Audience**
  ● Who is it aimed at?
  ● Consider: age, class, occupation, interests.

> You should be able to:
> ● compare the presentation of ideas, values or emotions in related or contrasting texts.

- **Language**
  - What kind of words are used – simple, complex/polysyllabic?
  - Consider the length of sentences and sentence construction.
  - Think about the use of jargon.
  - Is emotive language used?
- **Tone** – Is the article informative, shocking, humorous or sad?
- **Bias**
  - Is the article balanced or does it take sides?
  - Does the whole newspaper have a political bias?
- **Interviews** – Who has been interviewed and why?
- **Personal response** – How do you respond to this kind of reporting?

4.6 Reading for information and research

You should be able to:
- use appropriate reading strategies to extract particular information, e.g. highlighting, scanning.

When you read for **information**, you may use a range of reading techniques, depending on what you are reading and why you are reading it. There are three main types of reading: **scanning**, **skimming** and **intensive reading**.

Key Point

There are three kinds of reading for information: scanning, skimming and intensive reading.

Scanning

When you want to find a particular piece of information in a text, you may **scan read** for a **key word or phrase**. For example, if you want to know what time your favourite television programme is on, you don't need to read the TV listings magazine from cover to cover. Instead, you find the correct page for that day's television and scan the columns until you find the name of your television programme.

Use scanning to:
- **read timetables**
- find **keys words** and page references in an index
- find a **spelling** in a **dictionary**
- find a **number** in a **telephone directory**
- find the **relevant section** in a **leaflet**.

Once you have scanned a text, you may decide you need to read part of it more closely, e.g. the definition of the word you were looking for in the dictionary, or a summary of your favourite television programme.

Skimming

Skimming is a technique that allows you to read a whole text quickly, which can be very useful in exams. Skimming involves reading the whole text quickly to get a general understanding of what it is about and pick out key words and phrases.

- **For general reading and research** – this technique will help you to decide whether a text has the information you are looking for. You may then decide to read all or part of the text paying closer attention to detail.

- **In an exam** – the text will definitely be relevant to the task you have been set. This reading technique will help you to identify the important sections that you will need to read more closely. Once you have skimmed the text, read the questions carefully. Then you will be able to **skim** and **scan** for the key words and sections you need to answer each question.

> You should be able to:
> - appraise the value and relevance of information found and acknowledge sources.

Intensive reading

Once you have identified that fact that a text has the information you require, you need to read the relevant sections more carefully. **Intensive reading** allows you to gain the maximum information from a text. For general reading and research you should:

- read more **slowly**
- **check** definitions of words you don't understand
- **re-read** sentences or groups of sentences that express complex ideas
- make decisions about exactly what is **relevant** to your research
- **make notes or answer questions** based on the information you have learned – **don't copy from the text** unless you are quoting an example or you have been explicitly instructed to copy.

In an exam you should try to follow the same guidelines. However, you will have a time limit and you may not be allowed to check definitions – **you are not allowed to take dictionaries into many exams**.

Progress
Check

1. What kind of reading technique would you use to find a place on a map or in an atlas? **scanning/skimming/intensive reading**
2. Skim reading can completely replace intensive reading in an exam. TRUE or FALSE?
3. When you make notes you should always copy directly from the text you have read. TRUE or FALSE?

1 scanning 2 false 3 false

Practice test questions

The following questions will help you to prepare for Optional Tests in Years 7 and 8.

■ Ordeal of the long-distance runner... Robert in Caracus, Venezuela

Robert's one Gump ahead in long run

BY NICK WEBSTER

ROUND-the-world runner Robert Garside is set to bring the fictional hero Forest Gump alive for the American people.

After already running more than 25,000 miles across Australia, Asia, Europe and South America during his three-and-a-half year journey the former Stockport psychology student is due to reach the US border from Mexico on Thursday.

There the adventurer known as the Running Man is expected to be joined on the road by thousands of ordinary people as he makes his way from Los Angeles and San Francisco to New York on the east coast.

In the blockbuster film Forest Gump, Tom Hanks played the hero whose feats included running across the United States.

Robert, 33, who attended Hillcrest Grammar School, Stockport, and who still has relatives in Denton, has set his heart on running his way into the Guinness Book of Records.

But the incredible journey is not without its risks – Russian bandits have shot at him, thugs robbed him in Pakistan, in China he was jailed as a spy and only days ago he was mugged yet again and robbed of all his possessions in Mexico.

After leaving North America his epic trip will take him through Africa and Antartica. His progress can be followed on the Internet at http://runningman.org/

1 How old is Robert Garside? [1]

2 Which paragraph gives information about the dangers of his journey? [1]

3 Name **two** layout features used in this newspaper article. [2]

4 Which sentence is the topic sentence? [1]

5 Explain why the words *epic* and *hero* have been used. [2]

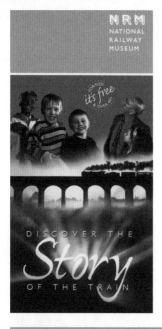

The following question will help you prepare for SATs in Year 9.

Assessment: AT2

Read the National Railway Museum leaflet below and look closely at the layout of the leaflet.

How does the writer of this leaflet try to inform people and persuade them to visit the museum?

Think about:

- the content of the leaflet
- particular words and phrases that are used
- layout

Marks: 6

Looking for a fun-packed, family day out, where entry is free for the under 17s and over 60s? Then why not come along to the National Railway Museum in York? It's the largest railway museum in the world!

Here, you'll experience the incredible story of the train as you've never seen or heard it before. You'll be amazed at how much we have to offer for a truly memorable journey through the past and into the present.

Rocket to Eurostar
See our replica of Stephenson's *Rocket*, the 172 year old engine responsible for reshaping the future of the steam locomotive. And the world record-breaking *Mallard* - its amazing steam speed record of 126 mph still stands

to this day. Contrast this with the sleek, streamlined shape of *Eurostar*. Its futuristic design reflects the state-of-the-art journey it makes every day, deep beneath the Channel. Or catch the technologically advanced Japanese Bullet train *Shinkansen*, as it goes on permanent display from 14 July.

Royal Coaches and Exhibitions
With the finest collection of Royal coaches in the world, dating back to before the Victorian era, you'll be amazed at how monarchs travelled in our *Palaces on Wheels* exhibition. And see how we deliver the story of the mail in *Moving Things - The Mail* via touch-screen technology, a karaoke machine and a push-button quiz.

5 Plan, draft and present

After studying this section you should be able to:

- plan a piece of writing
- draft and redraft a piece of writing
- present a piece of non-fiction writing

5.1 Planning

Brainstorming

Brainstorming is a good way to start any piece of writing.

- Write down as many ideas, **key words** and feelings as you can about the subject you need to write about.
- As soon as you have an idea, write it down.
- Don't worry about your handwriting or presentation.
- Use the best ideas in your final piece of writing.

Go for five

This technique will help you with descriptive or narrative writing. Try to think of **five** words or phrases for each pre-decided category. For example: **describing a scary forest**.

- **Sounds**: crunching, twigs snapping, shuffling, animals howling. . .
- **Textures**: crumbly moss, rough bark, sharp scratching thorns, ghostly cobwebs brushing my face. . .
- **Sights**: eerie shadows, shapes moving in the darkness, branches like hands reaching out to grab me, pin points of light like eyes. . .

Spider diagrams and brain maps

You could use a **spider diagram** to **brainstorm** your ideas about a character, storyline, memory, event or issue.

Write the central idea or issue in the centre of your page and then branch out from the centre like spider legs with the rest of your ideas. For example, use a spider diagram to brainstorm both sides of an argument about whether schools should have uniform. An example of this is shown on page 76.

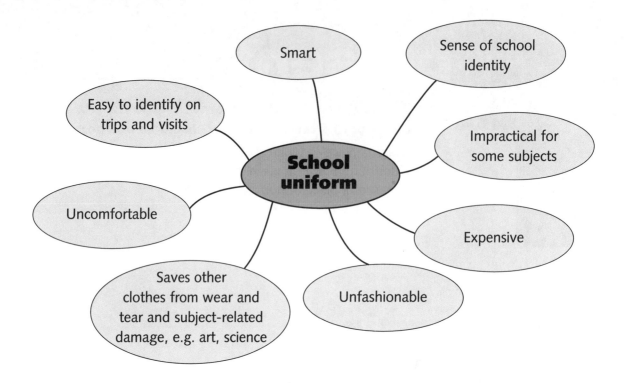

A **brain map** is similar to a **spider diagram**, but it allows you to organise your thoughts more clearly by putting in **extra layers**. If you were making a brain map to explore the different aspects of a character in a novel, you might present it like this:

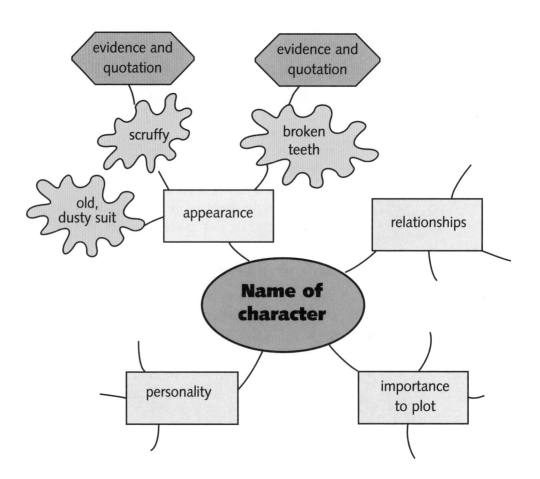

Making notes in a table or chart

Look back at the spider diagram about school uniform. As this brainstorm is looking at two sides of an argument, it may have been more usefully presented in a table.

School Uniform	
FOR	**AGAINST**
Sense of school identity Smart Easy to identify on trips and visits Saves other clothes from wear and tear and subject-related damage, e.g. art, science	Uncomfortable Expensive Unfashionable Impractical for some subjects

Key Point

As you work through the writing chapters you will find more advice about planning and examples of planning formats.

Formal planning

Before beginning an extended piece of writing, it is helpful to make a formal **paragraph plan**.

- **Non-fiction**: decide on the topic of each paragraph and write several bullet points to cover in each one.
- **Fiction**: decide how your story will develop and write several bullet points to show how each section of the plot will unfold.

5.2 Drafting and redrafting

Most major pieces of writing you do at school will be **drafted** and **redrafted**. This means you have a chance to refine and improve your ideas and the way you express them.

First draft

When writing your first draft, follow these guidelines.
- **Follow your plan**.
- **Concentrate** and try to write quite **quickly** in order to get into the rhythm of your writing.
- If you are unhappy with a word or phrase that you've used, **underline** it so that you can come back to it when you **redraft**.

Redrafting

If you are asked to **redraft** a piece of writing this doesn't mean you should copy it out in your best handwriting, although **neatness and legibility** are important. There are many things to look out for when you are redrafting.

Openings

It is important to grab the reader's interest straightaway. In an exam, you need to make sure the examiner can tell immediately that you understand what you've been asked to do. Think about changing **vocabulary or sentence structure** to make the opening more powerful.

Main Content

- Ensure that you have used a **range of sentence structures** in your writing to **vary the pace and create rhythms**.
- Ensure that you have made some **original** and **adventurous vocabulary** choices.
- Ensure that any **imagery is creative** and **original**.
- Check that you have **backed up your opinions** with **evidence and/or quotations**.

Proof reading

Proof reading is the process of re-reading a piece of writing to check the technical accuracy of your writing.

Spelling

- **Check** for any words you may have **misspelt** because you were writing in a hurry.
- **Check** words that you sometimes find confusing, e.g. **common homophones: there, their, they're**.
- **Underline** any words that you are unsure of and use a dictionary to check your spelling.

Remember, you can't use a dictionary in exams.

Punctuation

- Make sure you have used **capital letters** where they are needed.
- Check your use of **apostrophes**.
- Check punctuation in **complex sentences**.
- Read your work out loud to makes sure that your **punctuation helps the sense** of your writing.

Paragraphing

Remember that paragraphs are organised by **time**, **topic** or **talk**. Read through your work and make sure that your ideas are correctly organised into paragraphs.

> **Key Point**
>
> In an exam situation you don't have time for redrafting, but you should always make time for proof reading.

5.3 Presentation

The presentation of your final draft is very important. If your work is attractively presented, it will impress your teacher or examiner and give you a sense of pride in your own achievement.

Handwriting

Legible handwriting is important in school and in later life. It ensures that your meaning is expressed clearly and is easily understood. Neat and legible handwriting will encourage the reader to pay closer attention to what you have written.

Typing and word processing

Lots of students have access to computers to produce homework and extended written assignments. Although not compulsory, this helps to ensure that presentation is attractive and legible. If you do use a computer to present your work, think about the following points.

- Make sure that the **font style** and **size** is legible and appropriate to the task.
- Make use of facilities such as **bold type**, **underlining** and **bullet points**, but don't overdo these.
- Don't feel obliged to use all the presentational devices available with the software you are using, e.g. cartoon clip art isn't appropriate in a formal essay or letter.

> **Key Point**
>
> As you will have to write exam answers by hand, take time to practise writing at speed to make sure that your handwriting remains legible.

Presenting non-fiction texts

If you are asked to write a non-fiction text that uses different presentational devices, such as **columns, pictures, bullet points** and **different font sizes**, try to use these devices in your own writing.

If you are writing this kind of text in an exam, **don't waste time** with unnecessary **presentation**. For example, if you are writing a leaflet and want to include pictures, don't spend time drawing and colouring in. Instead, draw a box on the page where you would place a picture and write what the picture would show inside.

6 Writing to imagine, explore, entertain

After studying this section you should be able to:

- create believable characters when writing stories and poems
- create realistic and atmospheric settings for stories and poems
- use dialogue to create atmosphere and develop characters
- give your stories and poems a suitable structure
- structure your narrative and experiment with different narrative perspectives

To achieve the following National Curriculum levels you need to

Level 4
- think of an interesting storyline
- organise your ideas to hold the interest of the reader

Level 5
- experiment with figurative language
- create believable characters
- use language and structure to create atmosphere

Level 6
- maintain a balance of plot, description and dialogue
- vary the pace by using a range of sentence structures

Level 7
- sustain and develop characters and settings in narrative
- experiment with and control a range of narrative styles

6.1 Writing poetry

Personification

You should be able to:
- make links between your reading of fiction, plays and poetry and the choices you make as a writer.

Re-read the poem 'City Jungle' on page 41. To write a similar poem using **personification**, follow these instructions.

Plan

Think of a place: the beach.

Think of six **nouns** you would find at that place:

- sand dunes
- deck chairs
- clouds
- ice cream
- waves
- beach ball.

Think of six **verbs** you would associate with human beings:

Match up the **nouns and verbs**:

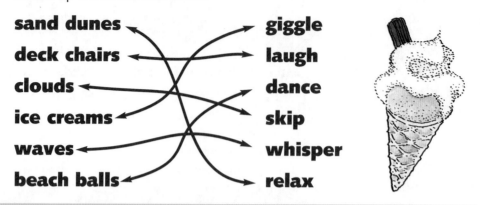

sand dunes → giggle

deck chairs → laugh

clouds → dance

ice creams → skip

waves → whisper

beach balls → relax

Key Point
- Alliteration – the repetition of a letter or letter sound at the beginning of a sequence of words.
- Noun phrase – a group of words with a noun as the central component.

Write

- Think about the best order in which to present these ideas and images.
- Add **adjectives** and **adverbs** to each phrase to create **extended noun phrases**.
- Try to use other devices such as **alliteration** in your poem.

> Brightly coloured bouncing beach balls dance along the shore.
> Fluffy white clouds skip lightly across the sky.
> Sparkling white-tipped waves whisper their secrets to chattering sea shells.
> Stripy deck chairs laugh at giggling, dripping ice creams.
> Sand dunes relax in the sun.

Redraft

- Think about the **shape** of your poem.
- Make decisions about **rhyme and rhythm**.
- Change or add **vocabulary**.

> Brightly coloured bouncing beach balls
> dance along the shore.
> Fluffy white **candyfloss** clouds
> skip lightly across the sky.
> Sparkling ~~white~~-**silver**-tipped waves
> whisper their secrets to chattering sea shells.
> Stripy deck chairs laugh at giggling, dripping ice creams.
> Sand dunes ~~relax~~ **blush** in the **setting** sun

- This poem doesn't have a regular rhyme scheme or rhythm – the personification that runs through the poem acts like the 'glue' which holds it together.
- The shape of the poem is supposed to be like the waves lapping on the shore.

1 What device, other than personification, is used in lines 1, 5 and 6?

2 Identify the adverb in line 4.

3 Why have the ideas about the deckchairs and the ice creams been joined together?

1 alliteration 2 lightly 3 Because they are both about laughter.

Have a go

Have a go at writing a personification poem about a fairground, a supermarket or your school.

6.2 Creating characters

If you are to create believable characters, you need to know them really well before you start writing. One way to get to know your characters is to create a **fact file**.

Fact file

Name:	Jamie Monks
Age:	15
Occupation:	student at local comprehensive, on the verge of exclusion
Appearance:	short brown hair, faded highlights; blue eyes, angry stare; school uniform always untidy, wears trainers even though it's against the rules; wears baggy skate clothes outside school
Personality:	appears to be a trouble maker and rule breaker; rebellious; teachers think he's disrespectful; good sense of humour, always making friends laugh; low self-esteem, doesn't think he can do or achieve anything; very kind to younger sister
Leisure/hobbies:	everything to do with skateboarding; listening to music (too loud!); being with friends
Ambition:	to win a major skateboarding competition
Fears:	failure – often refuses to attempt new things to avoid failure; turning out like his dad
Family:	lives with mum and younger sister, Allie; dad has left the home – mum always complains that Jamie is just like his dad but never explains what she means
Past/secret:	trying to find his dad, doesn't want mum to know as it will upset her

Character description

What kind of character fact file do you think this person would have?

> Mr Sugden was passing slowly across one end of the room, looking down the corridors and counting the boys as they changed. He was wearing a violet tracksuit. The top was embellished with cloth badges depicting numerous crests and qualifications, and on the breast a white athlete carried the Olympic torch. The legs were tucked into new white football socks, neatly folded at his ankles, and his football boots were polished as black and shiny as the bombs used by assassins in comic strips. The laces binding them had been scrubbed white, and both boots had been fastened identically: two loops of the foot and one of the ankle, and tied in a neat bow under the tab at the back.
>
> From *A Kestrel for a Knave* by Barry Hines

You should be able to:
- portray character, directly and indirectly, through description, dialogue and action.

Does this description of Mr Sugden help you to understand the way he behaves in the extract on pages 22–23, and why he dislikes Billy?

Key Point

It isn't possible or desirable to reveal everything about a character through explicit description – some of the information about the character should be implied. Give your reader clues about characters from the way they behave, what they say and how they say it.

There are more examples of character descriptions in Chapter 2 Reading fiction and plays.

Word level

Try to experiment with figurative language. In the description of Mr Sugden, the writer uses a simile: *his football boots were polished as black and shiny as the bombs used by assassins in comic strips*. This links Mr Sugden to danger, but it also gives the impression that the author finds the character a bit foolish and comical.

Key Point

Once you have made a character fact file, you should keep it as a reference to make sure that your character behaves in a believable way throughout the story.

Progress Check

1 You should reveal everything about a character directly. TRUE or FALSE?
2 Mr Sugden doesn't care about his appearance. TRUE or FALSE?
3 The image used to describe Mr Sugden's football boots is a simile/metaphor.

1 false   2 false   3 simile

Have a Go

1 Write a character fact file of your own.
2 Write a short description of that character.
3 Write a short passage about your character, involving action and dialogue to give clues and implied character information to the reader.

6.3 Creating a setting

Creating real places

When you are writing a story, **realistic locations** are just as important as believable characters.

A few miles south of Soledad, the Salinas River drops in close to the hill-side bank and runs deep and green. The water is warm too, for it has slipped twinkling over the yellow sands in the sunlight before reaching the narrow pool. On one side of the river the golden foothill slopes curve up to the strong and rocky Gabilan mountains, but on the valley side the water is lined with trees – willows fresh and green with every spring, carrying in their lower leaf junctures the debris of the winter's flooding; and sycamores with mottled, white, recumbent limbs and branches that arch over the pool. On the sandy bank under the trees the leaves lie deep and so crisp that a lizard makes a great skittering if he runs among them. Rabbits come out of the brush to sit on the sand in the evening, and the damp flats are covered with the night tracks of 'coons, and with the spread pads of dogs from the ranches, and with the split-wedge tracks of deer that come to drink in the dark.

From *Of Mice and Men* by John Steinbeck

In **science fiction** and **fantasy** stories, locations still have to be believable settings for the action taking place there.

That had only taken it as far as the general bay engineering space, the biggest single volume in the ship with the divisions down; nine thousand metres deep, nearly twice that across and filled with noise and flickering lights and blurringly fast motion as the ship created thousands of new machines to do . . . who-knew-what.

Most of the engineering space wasn't even filled with air; the material, components and machines could move faster that way. Gravious was flying down a transparent traveltube set into the ceiling. Nine kilometres of that took it to a wall which led into the relative serenity – or at least, stillness – of the sea battle tableau. It was half way across that now; just another four thousand metres to go.

From *Excession* by Iain M Banks

Atmosphere

You should be able to:
- experiment with figurative language in conveying a sense of character and setting.

You can create a particular **atmosphere** through your description of the **setting** of a story. To create atmosphere you need to think carefully about the **vocabulary**, **imagery** and **sentence structure** you use in your writing. Look at the following descriptions of a beach and decide what kind of atmosphere is being created.

Dark, brooding clouds bruised the sky. Rain battered the cliffs. The wind howled as if in pain, filling my brain with the terrible memories of my last visit to the beach.

Wispy clouds scudded across the sun as the wind whipped playfully against deckchair canvas.

The sun smiled down from a bright, cloudless sky. Children's laughter mingled with the lively shouts of excited seagulls.

Creating tension and suspense

Read the following extract and think about how character description and behaviour, use of language and structure help to create **tension**.

The narrator begins very confidently, but by the end of the extract he begins to sound doubtful.

repeated warnings

formal, old fashioned and complicated style of speech gives clues about the character – pompous and arrogant

early clues that the house is haunted

unpleasant character description

repeated descriptive detail

'I can assure you,' said I, 'that it will take a very tangible ghost to frighten me.' And I stood up before the fire with my glass in my hand.

'It is your own choosing,' said the man with the withered arm, and glanced at me askance.

'Eight-and-twenty years,' said I, 'I have lived, and never a ghost have I seen as yet.'

The old woman sat staring hard into the fire, her pale eyes wide open. 'Ah,' she broke in: 'and eight-and-twenty years you have lived and never seen the likes of this house, I reckon. There's a many things to see, when one's still but eight-and-twenty.' She swayed her head slowly from side to side. 'A many thing to see and sorrow for.'

I half suspected the old people were trying to enhance the spiritual terrors of their house by their droning insistence. I put down my empty glass on the table and looked about the room, and caught a glimpse of myself, abbreviated and broadened to an impossible sturdiness, in the queer old mirror at the end of the room. 'Well,' I said, 'if I see anything tonight, I shall be so much the wiser. For I come to the business with an open mind.'

'It's your own choosing,' said the man with the withered arm once more.

I heard the sound of a stick and a shambling step on the flags in the passage outside, and the door creaked on its hinges as a second old man entered, more bent, more wrinkled, more aged even than the first. He supported himself by a single crutch, his eyes were covered by a shade, and his lower lip, half averted, hung pale and pink from his decaying yellow teeth. He made straight for an armchair on the opposite side of the table, sat down clumsily, and began to cough. The man with the withered arm gave this newcomer a short glance of positive dislike; the old woman took no notice of his arrival, but remained with her eyes fixed steadily on the fire.

'I said – it's your own choosing,' said the man with the withered arm, when the coughing had ceased for a while.

'It's my own choosing,' I answered.

The man with the shade became aware of my presence for the first time, and threw his head back for a moment and sideways, to see me. I caught a momentary glimpse of his eyes, small and bright and inflamed. Then he began to cough and splutter again.

'Why don't you drink?' said **the man with the withered arm**, pushing the beer towards him. The man with the shade poured out a glassful with a shaky arm that splashed half as much again on the deal table. A **monstrous shadow of him crouched upon the wall and mocked his action as he poured and drank. I must confess I had scarce expected these grotesque custodians.**

From *The Red Room* by H G Wells

> description that emphasises the dim lighting and shadows

Glossary

tangible – real

askance – to look with suspicion or disapproval

enhance the spiritual terrors – exaggerate the ghostly nature of the house

averted – hidden

custodians – caretakers

> You should be able to:
> - use a range of narrative devices to involve the reader, e.g. *withholding information.*

One of the most successful techniques H G Wells has used in this passage is **withholding information**. The reader doesn't really know who these people are, where they are or what they are doing there. This forces the reader to predict what will happen and allows the reader to be involved in the story straightaway.

Sentence level

The National Literacy Strategy requires you to: **recognise some of the differences in sentence structure, vocabulary and tone between a modern English text and a text from another historical period.** Some obvious examples from *The Red Room* are:

'Eight-and-twenty years,' said I – the tone of this speech is very formal. This is because of the word order (syntax). In modern speech we would say or write: 'Twenty-eight years,' I said.

I put down my empty glass on the table and looked about the room, and caught a glimpse of myself, abbreviated and broadened to an impossible sturdiness, in the queer old mirror at the end of the room. In modern writing there is a trend towards shorter sentences and the use of fewer commas. The above sentence could be expressed as a compound sentence followed by a complex sentence, rather than just one complicated complex sentence: 'I put down my glass and looked about the room. I caught a glimpse...'

Progress Check

1 Syntax is the technical term for what?

2 'Dark, brooding clouds bruised the sky.' is a **complex/compound/simple** sentence.

3 The sentence in question 2 uses personification. TRUE or FALSE?

1 word order 2 simple 3 true

6.4 Writing dialogue

Dialogue is another word for **speech** or **conversation**. Most fiction contains dialogue because it allows the main characters to communicate with each other. Dialogue is important for the following reasons:

- it helps to **bring the characters to life**
- it **reveals new information** about the character speaking or the character being spoken about
- it **adds variety** to the story.

It is important to think about **how** characters say things, as well as **what** they say.

When you use dialogue in a story, think about all the different ways there are to describe **how** somebody says something. Using a variety of verbs to describe speech gives the reader more information about what a character is like. Here are some words you could use to replace **said**.

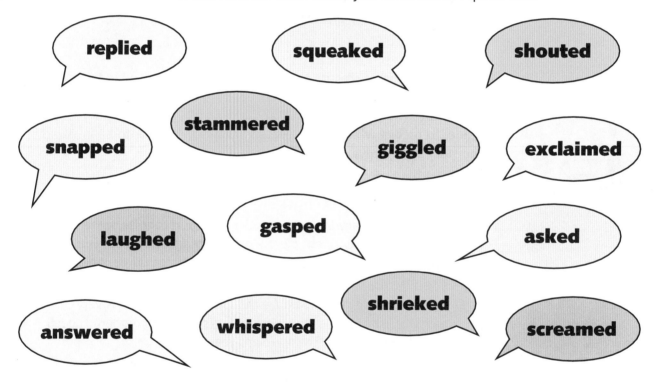

replied   squeaked   shouted
snapped   stammered   giggled   exclaimed
laughed   gasped   asked
answered   whispered   shrieked   screamed

6.5 Structure

You should be able to:

- structure a story with an **arresting opening**, a developing plot, a complication, a crisis and a satisfying resolution.

Your writing needs a clearly defined structure. This will usually take the form of three definite stages: **the beginning**, **the middle** and **the ending**.

The beginning

- In the opening section of a piece of imaginative writing, you need to introduce the **characters** and the **setting** and begin to **develop the main plot strands**.
- It is important to **create an interesting opening**, as you need to capture the attention of your reader.

- Do not give your reader too much detail. Keep them guessing so that they will want to read on. **Never launch straight into 'telling a story'.**
- Begin with an interesting **description of a character or the setting**.
- If you are writing a **first-person narrative**, you could begin with an intriguing statement from the narrator.

Key Point

If you can handle a more complicated structure, you could begin the story with the climax of the plot and go on to look at how the events took place. You could produce a circular structure by returning to the same event at the end.

The following extract, from *Kit's Wilderness* by David Almond, serves as a prologue to the main story. This opening refers to the end of the story, which gives the book a **circular structure**. It is an effective opening because it raises questions, gives the reader clues about what will happen in the story and introduces the main characters in an intriguing way.

> **They thought we had disappeared, and they were wrong. They thought we were dead, and they were wrong.** We stumbled together out of the ancient darkness into the shining valley. The sun glared down on us. The whole world glistened with ice and snow. We held our arms against the light and stared in wonder at each other. **We were scorched and blackened from the flames. There was dried blood on our lips, cuts and bruises on our skin.** Our eyes began to burn with joy and we laughed, and touched each other and started to walk down together towards Stoneygate. Down there, our neighbours were digging for us in the snow. Policemen were dragging the river bed for us. The children saw us first and started running. Their voices echoed with astonishment and joy: 'Here they are! Oh, here they are!' They clustered around us. **They watched us as if we were ghosts, or creatures from some weird dream.** 'Here they are!' they whispered. 'Look at them. Look at the state of them!'
>
> Yes, here we were, the children who had disappeared, brought back into the world as if by magic: **John Askew, the blackened boy with bone necklaces and paintings on him; Allie Keenan, the good-bad ice girl with silver skin and claws; the wild dog Jax; and me, Kit Watson, with ancient stories in my head and ancient pebbles in my palm.**
>
> We kept on walking towards our homes with the children whispering and giggling at our side. We smiled and smiled. **Who could have known that we would walk together with such happiness, after all we'd been through? At times it seemed that there would be no end it, that there would just be darkness, that there would be no light. It started with a game, a game we played in the autumn. I played it first on the day the clocks went back.**
>
> *From Kit's Wilderness by David Almond*

Annotations (margin notes):

Clue: the main characters go missing and are presumed dead.

Question: what has happened to them?

Clue: the whole community has been searching and worrying

Intriguing introduction to and description of the main characters.
Clues: Kit is the narrator. The story is connected to the past

Questions: What is the game? What have they been through?

Clues: the game will be important.

Opening sentences

The opening sentences of this example are particularly effective:

They thought we had disappeared, and they were wrong. They thought we were dead, and they were wrong.

These two sentences have exactly the same structure.

Repetition of *they* and *we* suggests a battle or misunderstanding between the main characters and the community.

The sentences would make sense without the comma, but the comma emphasises the differences between 'them' and 'us'.

References to disappearance and death make the opening dramatic and powerful and raise questions immediately.

> The comma creates a caesura.

The middle

- In the central section of your writing, you need to **develop plot, characterisation and relationships**. Development is essential if you are to hold the interest of the reader.
- If you made a **character fact file** as preparation, make sure you introduce some details from it.
- **Refer back** to your character plans to make sure that they react to events in the way their personalities suggest. If you have said that a character is selfish and self-obsessed, he or she wouldn't offer to help a stranger.
- Think about how you can use **language and structure** to make your writing interesting and lively.

Plot, description and dialogue

Make sure you keep a **balance between plot development, dialogue (conversation) and description**. Too much dialogue makes your writing stilted. (Remember, you are not writing a script!)

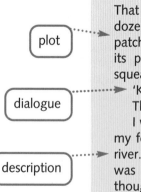

plot — That day after school I went out alone, climbed the fence. There were dozens of kids playing in the gathering dark. There was a slide on a bare patch of ground. Someone had brought a lantern down. They slid through its pale glow, clashed into each other, went sprawling, laughed and squealed.

dialogue — 'Kit!' someone yelled. 'Come and play, Kit!'
Then screamed: 'Aaaaaaaa! Hahaha!'

description — I waved and walked on. The frosted grass crunched and crackled under my feet. The houselights from the opposite bank shimmered on the slow river. Stars brightened as the dark came on. No moon. I looked down and was certain I saw ice forming there at the river's edge. Cold enough, I thought. Bitter cold.
I closed my eyes, saw Grandpa as a boy, slipping and sliding on the ice. I smiled to myself, then heard a whispering, a tiny giggling nearby. Opened my eyes, saw nothing.

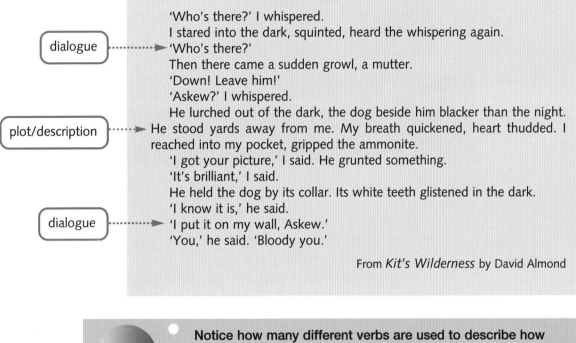

dialogue

'Who's there?' I whispered.
I stared into the dark, squinted, heard the whispering again.
'Who's there?'
Then there came a sudden growl, a mutter.
'Down! Leave him!'
'Askew?' I whispered.
He lurched out of the dark, the dog beside him blacker than the night.

plot/description

He stood yards away from me. My breath quickened, heart thudded. I reached into my pocket, gripped the ammonite.
'I got your picture,' I said. He grunted something.
'It's brilliant,' I said.
He held the dog by its collar. Its white teeth glistened in the dark.
'I know it is,' he said.

dialogue

'I put it on my wall, Askew.'
'You,' he said. 'Bloody you.'

From *Kit's Wilderness* by David Almond

Key Point

- Notice how many different verbs are used to describe how things are said: yelled, screamed, whispered.
- Sometimes you don't need to add he said/she said; this helps to maintain the rhythm of the conversation.

The ending

In the final section of your writing, you must begin to tie up loose ends. You have three main options for finishing your writing:

- **a cliffhanger**
- **a twist in the tale**
- **a resolution.**

Cliffhanger

With a cliffhanger, the story ends **without conclusion** or **resolution**. This keeps the reader guessing as to what will happen next. However, you need to **leave some clues** and have some ideas yourself about what will happen next. You should **plan** to finish in this way rather than realising you have run out of time. An unfinished ending and a cliffhanger ending are two completely different things!

Twist in the tale

A twist in the tale is a completely **unexpected** twist in the plot, right at the end. This is an exciting way to end a story but it is also more difficult to manage. Again, it is important to **plan** for this kind of ending.

Resolution

With a resolution, all the loose ends are tied up and the ending is **complete and definite**. This would often be a happy ending, but it doesn't have to be.

Try to avoid clichéd endings. You could really ruin a good story for want of an original conclusion. For example avoid, 'Then I woke up. It had all been a dream!'

Key Point

Time spent planning is time well spent. In an exam situation you should take between five and ten minutes to think about **what** you are going to write and **how** you are going to sustain your narrative. You should also plan how your story is going to end.

Progress Check

1 Dialogue is another word for...
2 You should develop plot, characterisation and relationships at the **beginning/middle/ending** of a story.
3 A story that ends without resolution is a **cliffhanger/twist in the tale** ending.

1 conversation   **2** middle   **3** cliffhanger

Have a go
Plan the structure for a story about a journey to a new and unfamiliar place.
1 Write the opening sentences.
2 Decide on which kind of ending you will use.
3 Write five main bullet points for each section. Think about: **characters, setting, plot developments, relationship developments and language.**

6.6 Narrative perspective

You should be able to:
- explore different ways of opening, structuring and ending narratives and experiment with narrative perspective.

It is possible to manipulate the reader by experimenting with different **narrative voices**.

Third-person narrative

In **third-person narrative**, the narrator is someone who is outside the story and refers to all the characters by name or he/she. This style of narration allows you to show more than one perspective.

An **omniscient narrator** is a narrator who knows everything about the situations and characters (and their feelings) in a story. This allows the narrator to let the reader into the inner thoughts and feelings of the characters and to comment on them. It also means that the narrator can give information about what will happen later in the story so that the **reader knows more than the characters.**

First-person narrative

First-person narrative usually looks at situations from only one point of view. This means that the narrator can **manipulate** the reader's sympathies by emphasising particular aspects of a story or leaving out information. A first-person narrator can be somebody who relates a story as they have observed it, a minor participant in the story they are relating, or a central character in the story. Kit Watson is the narrator and central character in *Kit's Wilderness*.

Dual narrative

The following extract is from a novel called *Stone Cold* by Robert Swindells. In this novel there is a **dual narrative**: the same story is told by Link, a homeless teenager and Shelter, a psychopathic killer who targets homeless people. Placing the **two stories side by side** shows two contrasting points of view on the same subject. As the story progresses, the characters and their stories sometimes meet and start to weave together and then diverge again. This is effective because it shows the danger that the unsuspecting Link is in.

According to Link and his friend Ginger, **solcredulists** are people who believe everything they read in *The Sun*.

For something to do, I began studying their various responses. Some would simply walk on glassy-eyed and expressionless, as though Ginger wasn't there. Some assumed angry expressions, compressing their lips and sweeping by as though grossly insulted. There were head-shakers, pocket-patters and shruggers, who demonstrated through mime the absence of coins in their pockets; and there were those who'd mutter unintelligibly, so that you couldn't tell whether they'd said sorry no change or bugger off. Once Ginger accosted a stiff, military-looking guy who stopped, looked him up and down as if he was something the cat sicked up and said, 'Change? I'd change you my lad, if I had you in khaki for six weeks.' There were a lot of **solcredulists** about.

Daily Routine Orders 8

It has happened again. I was on my way to inspect theatreland when two dossers approached me. One – the scruffier of the two – asked me for change. I responded in my usual way, and as I passed on I distinctly heard them laughing. I hope for their sakes that they manage to retain that sense of humour because they'll need it quite soon. I never forget a face, and our next meeting will prove far more amusing for me than for them.

By golly it will.

From *Stone Cold* by Robert Swindells

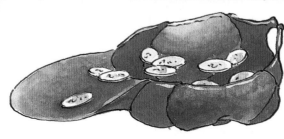

Word level

Omniscient means knowing everything.

The prefix omni- means all, from the Latin *omnis* meaning all: omnipotent – all powerful, omnivorous – feeds on many kinds of food.

Use a dictionary to check that the following words have something to do with all or everything: omnibus, omnidirectional, omnipresent.

Progress Check

1 In third-person narrative, the narrator takes part in the story. TRUE or FALSE?

2 A dual narrative tells the same story from more than one point of view. TRUE or FALSE?

3 Omniscient means: a) all powerful b) all knowing c) everywhere

1 false   2 true   3 b) all knowing

Have a go

Try writing the same story from different narrative perspectives. How does it change the story?

Practice test questions

The following question will help you to prepare for the Optional Tests in Years 7 and 8.

Time: 25 minutes

Assessment: AT3 writing

Lots of people believe in ghosts and the supernatural.

Write three or four paragraphs of a story including: dialogue, action, description of characters and setting to create a tense or frightening atmosphere.

Marks: 20

The following questions will help you to prepare for SATs in Year 9. The **Writing Paper** will be 1 hour and 15 minutes **including** planning time.

You will be required to complete **two** tasks which test your skills in two of the writing triplets. **Task one is 45 minutes** long and tests: sentence structure and punctuation, text structure and organisation, composition and effect. **Task two is 30 minutes** long and tests: sentence and text organisation, composition and effect, spelling.

These questions test your ability to write to **imagine**, **explore and entertain**, you should spend 45 minutes answering each question. **Remember**, in the exam you will only complete **one** 45 minute task.

1 'It wasn't me!'

Write about someone wrongly suspected or accused of committing a crime.

Think about:
- what they have been accused of
- how that person would feel
- what happens to them.

2 Write about a frightening encounter with an animal.
- Try to build up a feeling of tension or suspense.
- Describe the animal.

3 Write about being lost or followed in a forest.
- Try to build up an atmosphere of fear.
- Describe the forest.
- Write in the first or third person.

7 Writing to inform, instruct, explain and describe

After studying this section you should be able to:

- write to inform
- write to instruct
- write to explain
- write to describe

To achieve the following National Curriculum levels you need to

Level 4
- sustain and develop your ideas
- organise your ideas appropriately to suit a range of purposes

Level 5
- make your meaning clear in a range of forms
- use a more formal style where appropriate
- make adventurous vocabulary choices

Level 6
- use an impersonal style where appropriate
- use a range of sentence structures to create effects

Level 7
- consistently match your writing style to the purpose and audience of your writing
- use paragraphing and punctuation to make the sequence of ideas coherent to the reader

---

7.1 Writing to inform

Conventions of information texts

Information texts are written in the **present tense** and the **third person**. Sentences are usually **simple** and **compound** to present information in a straightforward way. Information texts use the following devices: **sub-headings, pictures, charts** and **tables**.

The text on page 97 conforms to most of the conventions of an information text.

Key Point Common information texts are: leaflets, textbooks and encyclopaedia entries.

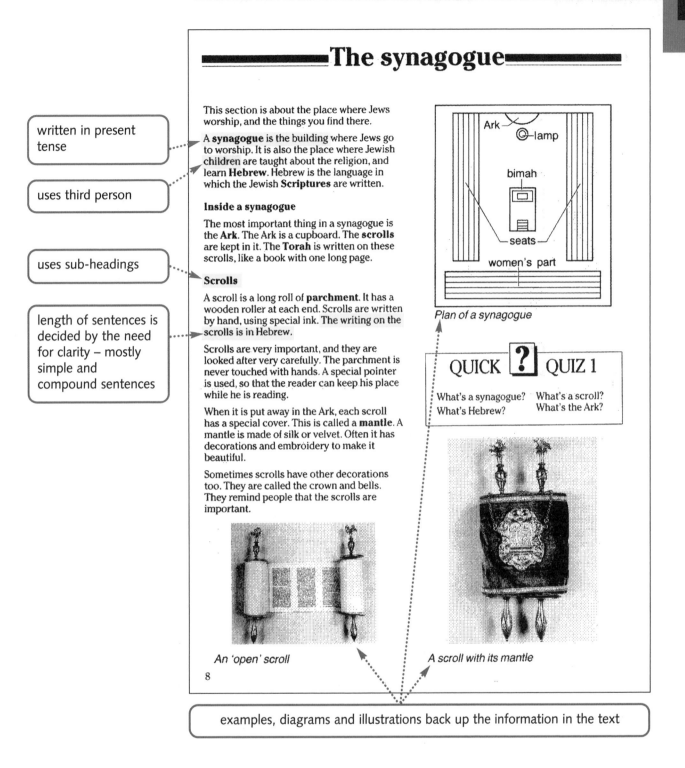

written in present tense

uses third person

uses sub-headings

length of sentences is decided by the need for clarity – mostly simple and compound sentences

The synagogue

This section is about the place where Jews worship, and the things you find there.

A **synagogue** is the building where Jews go to worship. It is also the place where Jewish children are taught about the religion, and learn **Hebrew**. Hebrew is the language in which the Jewish **Scriptures** are written.

Inside a synagogue

The most important thing in a synagogue is the **Ark**. The Ark is a cupboard. The **scrolls** are kept in it. The **Torah** is written on these scrolls, like a book with one long page.

Scrolls

A scroll is a long roll of **parchment**. It has a wooden roller at each end. Scrolls are written by hand, using special ink. The writing on the scrolls is in Hebrew.

Scrolls are very important, and they are looked after very carefully. The parchment is never touched with hands. A special pointer is used, so that the reader can keep his place while he is reading.

When it is put away in the Ark, each scroll has a special cover. This is called a **mantle**. A mantle is made of silk or velvet. Often it has decorations and embroidery to make it beautiful.

Sometimes scrolls have other decorations too. They are called the crown and bells. They remind people that the scrolls are important.

An 'open' scroll

8

Plan of a synagogue

Ark – lamp
bimah
seats
women's part

QUICK **?** QUIZ 1

What's a synagogue?   What's a scroll?
What's Hebrew?   What's the Ark?

A scroll with its mantle

examples, diagrams and illustrations back up the information in the text

Writing your own information text

You should be able to:

● organise and present information, selecting and synthesising appropriate material and guiding the reader clearly through the text.

There are three main steps to follow when writing your own information text. Follow these steps to write an information text about your school.

Planning

The first thing you need to do is to decide on the categories of information you are going to provide, for example by making a spider diagram like the one on the next page.

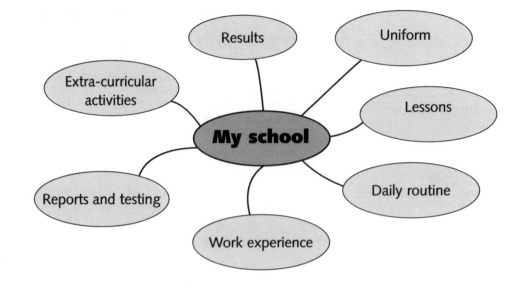

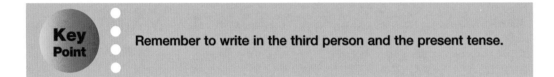

Key Point: Remember to write in the third person and the present tense.

Writing

Your writing style needs to be clear, factual and formal. As you are required to write in the third person, you should use terms such as: 'students study a wide range of subjects'. **Don't** use **we** or **I**: 'at school **we study** lots of different subjects'.

Look at this short example of writing about the lessons that take place in a particular school. Instead of giving this the title 'Lessons', you could use a more **formal** expression like 'The Curriculum'

The Curriculum
In Year 7, students follow a full programme of National Curriculum subjects, including Religious Education, Drama and ICT. In Years 8 and 9 students are given the opportunity to enhance their language skills by following courses in both French and German.

Visual variety

Remember that a successful information text needs to hold the reader's attention. Think about ways you can improve the visual impact of your information text:

- bullet points
- pictures
- headings
- different font sizes and styles
- colour
- tables, charts and graphs.

So, for example, when you are writing about your school you might present recent exam results in a graph or chart, and uniform details as a bullet pointed list, e.g.

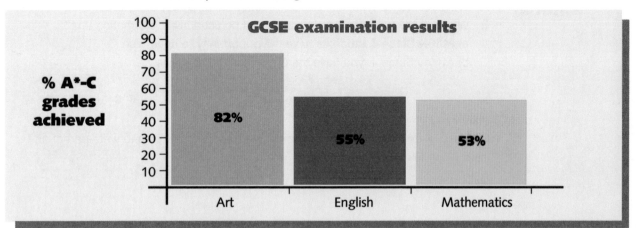

GCSE examination results

% A*-C grades achieved

- Art 82%
- English 55%
- Mathematics 53%

Lower School Girls Uniform
- Navy skirt
- White shirt
- Navy and gold school tie (ties may be bought from the school office)
- Plain navy v-neck jumper
- Navy blazer with school badge
- Navy tights or white socks

When does information become persuasion?

Volunteering...

...in your local Help the Aged shop

There are nearly 350 Help the Aged shops across England, Wales, Northern Ireland and Scotland. The shops raise funds by selling good quality donated clothes, books, bric-a-brac etc. Apart from finding a bargain or two, customers can also pick up Help the Aged leaflets which give helpful advice on issues affecting older people.

How You Can Help Us

Each shop has a paid manager, a deputy manager and a team of volunteer helpers. We are always looking for people who can spare a morning, afternoon or a full day each week to help out in their local shop.

What We Can Offer

Whatever your reasons for volunteering, we can guarantee a friendly working atmosphere and the opportunity to be an important part of a happy and dedicated team. You can become involved in all aspects of shop work; from sorting and pricing stock to operating a till, from window dressing to serving customers. There's never a dull moment!

Shops Volunteer Club

After three months, you will become a member of the *Shops Volunteer Club*. Benefits include a 20% discount in all the Help the Aged shops. Regular club meetings are held at which volunteers decide which social activities they would like to organise for their shop, with money from the *Volunteer Activity Fund*. This can be anything from a meal at a local restaurant to a day trip to the seaside!

Remember that many texts have more than one purpose. This means that information can sometimes be presented in a persuasive way. Read the example on the left; it is an information leaflet from 'Help the Aged'. As well as giving information about the charity, it clearly aims to persuade the people who read it to volunteer their help.

Progress Check

1 Which word in the following sentence indicates that it is written in the present tense? *Homework is an important part of the learning process.*
2 Which sentence type is least used in information texts? simple/complex
3 Which of the following sentences should be used in an information text?
  a) At Key Stage 4, students have the opportunity to specialise ...
  b) At Key Stage 4, you have the opportunity to specialise ...

1 is 2 complex 3 a)

Have a go

Choose one of the ideas from the spider diagram on page 98 and write part of an information text about your school.

7.2 Writing to instruct

Instruction texts include: directions, rules for playing games, recipes, manuals (DIY, etc.).

Giving clear instructions

Read the following description of how to make beans on toast. Is it a useful set of instructions for making beans on toast? If not, why not?

How to make beans on toast

I don't know much about cooking, but I can make beans on toast. The toast should be golden brown and really hot. You can cook the toast in a toaster or under the grill. I always burn my fingers on the grill, so I like to use the toaster – I love the noise it makes when it pops up! You can use butter or margarine on your toast, but I like butter best, especially if there are little air holes in the bread so the melted butter drips on your fingers – yum! I should have mentioned that while you are cooking your toast you need to cook the beans, otherwise your toast will be cold and soggy – yuck!! So put the beans in a saucepan and turn the heat up quite high. Of course, you need to take the beans out of the tin before you cook them. Make sure that you don't have too much heat because you should try not to boil or burn the beans. When they are hot enough – don't stick your finger in to test them because you could burn it – put the beans on the toast and enjoy!

There are many problems with this recipe. The main problems are:
- it is **disorganised**
- it is **difficult to follow** because it's all one paragraph and doesn't have clear steps
- it contains **personal opinion**
- it is too **conversational**.

This 'recipe' can't really be described as an instructional text as it breaks nearly all the rules listed below.

Conventions of instruction texts

Instruction texts:
- are written in the **imperative**
- are written in the **present tense**
- can include some sentences containing '**you**' but shouldn't use '**I**'
- have **short sentences**, each covering one instruction
- use **connectives** related to time or chronology, e.g. **then, next**
- punctuation is limited to **commas** and **full stops**
- don't contain personal information or anecdote (stories)
- don't use emotive language to describe the product
- are presented in **logical steps**, in **short paragraphs** that can be numbered
- often **begin with a list** of ingredients, materials, equipment
- include a **title or statement** of what is to be achieved.

Now read the following recipe. The way it is written makes it clearer and more effective.

> You should be able to:
> - write instructions which are helpfully sequenced and signposted and deploy a range of imperative verbs.

---

title →

list of ingredients →

Buttered Tagliatelle with Parmesan

250g (8 oz) tagliatelle, plain or verde

40g (15 oz) butter

salt and pepper

2 tablespoons grated Parmesan cheese, to serve

1 tablespoon chopped parsley, to garnish

written in imperative →

Cook the tagliatelle in plenty of boiling salted water for 5 minutes, or according to the packet instructions, **until al dente.**

connectives related to time

Drain the tagliatelle, rinse with hot water and drain again.

short sentences →

Melt the butter in the saucepan. Add the tagliatelle and toss to coat evenly with the butter.

Transfer the pasta to a warmed serving dish or individual dishes. Sprinkle with some pepper, Parmesan cheese and parsley and serve immediately.

punctuation limited to full stops and commas

clear, logical steps to follow →

Serves 4

Progress Check

1 Which punctuation mark should have been avoided in the beans on toast recipe?

2 When making beans on toast, you need to make the toast and cook the beans at the same time. Which of the following connectives would be most useful to explain this: **first, meanwhile, finally**?

3 Identify two imperative verbs in the recipe for Buttered Tagliatelle.

1 exclamation mark **2** meanwhile
3 cook, drain, rinse, melt, add, toss, transfer, sprinkle, serve

Have a go ...

Write your own recipe for making beans on toast.

7.3 Writing to explain

Conventions of an explanation text

The text below conforms to most of the conventions of an explanation text.

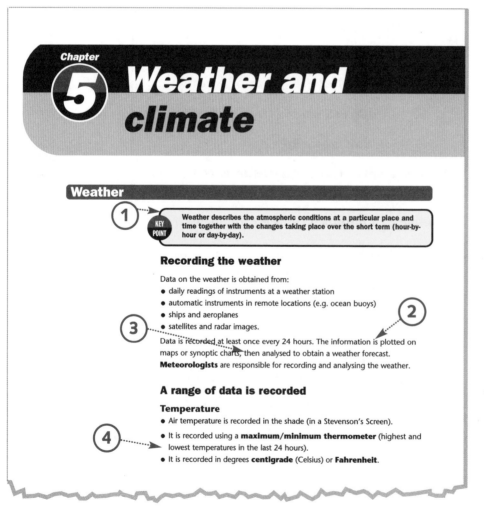

Chapter 5 Weather and climate

Weather

1 Weather describes the atmospheric conditions at a particular place and time together with the changes taking place over the short term (hour-by-hour or day-by-day).

Recording the weather

Data on the weather is obtained from:
- daily readings of instruments at a weather station
- automatic instruments in remote locations (e.g. ocean buoys)
- ships and aeroplanes
- satellites and radar images.

Data is recorded at least once every 24 hours. The information is plotted on maps or synoptic charts, then analysed to obtain a weather forecast.
Meteorologists are responsible for recording and analysing the weather.

A range of data is recorded

Temperature
- Air temperature is recorded in the shade (in a Stevenson's Screen).
- It is recorded using a **maximum/minimum thermometer** (highest and lowest temperatures in the last 24 hours).
- It is recorded in degrees **centigrade** (Celsius) or **Fahrenheit**.

1 The opening contains a **general statement** to introduce the topic.

2 The text uses the **passive voice**.

3 Uses **connectives** that indicate **sequence**.

4 The text is written in the **present tense**.

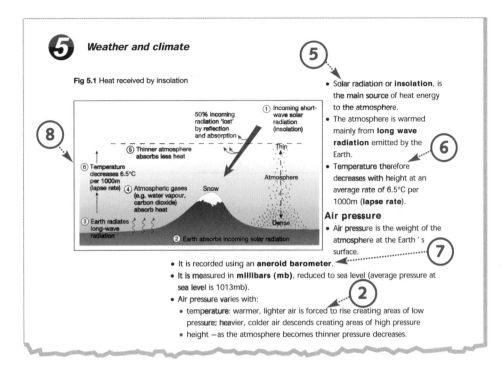

⑤ Weather and climate

Fig 5.1 Heat received by insolation

⑤

- Solar radiation or **insolation**, is the **main source** of heat energy to the **atmosphere**.
- The atmosphere is warmed mainly from **long wave radiation** emitted by the Earth.   **⑥**
- Temperature therefore decreases with height at an average rate of 6.5°C per 1000m (**lapse rate**).

Air pressure
- Air **pressure** is the weight of the atmosphere at the Earth's surface.   **⑦**
- It is recorded using an **aneroid barometer**.
- It is measured in **millibars (mb)**, reduced to sea level (average pressure at sea level is 1013mb).   **②**
- Air pressure varies with:
  - temperature: warmer, lighter air is forced to rise creating areas of low pressure; heavier, colder air descends creating areas of high pressure
  - height —as the atmosphere becomes thinner pressure decreases.

5 The development of the explanation draws attention to **how** something works or **why** something happens.

6 Uses **connectives** that indicate **cause and effect**.

7 **Technical vocabulary** gives the piece quite a formal style.

8 Uses **diagrams** to explain processes.

Connectives word bank

Use the following **connectives** in your own writing.

> You should be able to:
> - use a range of link words and phrases to signpost texts, including links of time *(then, later, meanwhile)* and cause *(so, because, since)*.

Cause and effect	**Sequence**	**Comparison**
because	then	similarly
so	next	whereas
due to	gradually	on the other hand
as a result of	finally	by contrast
therefore		however

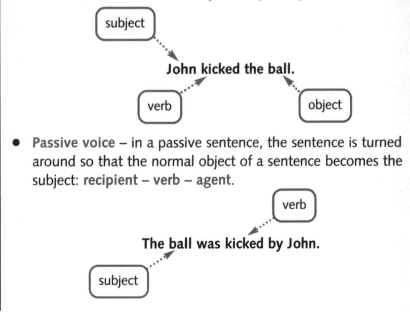

Sentence level
- **Active voice** – in an active sentence, the subject or agent performs the verb, which is received by the object: **agent – verb – recipient**.

  subject

  John kicked the ball.

  verb   object

- **Passive voice** – in a passive sentence, the sentence is turned around so that the normal object of a sentence becomes the subject: **recipient – verb – agent**.

  verb

  The ball was kicked by John.

  subject

Sentence level continued

The **active voice** is more common than the **passive voice**, which can sometimes seem clumsy or unnatural.

However, the passive voice can omit the agent, and this kind of sentence can be quite useful. Leaving out the agent allows the writer to conceal who is responsible for an action, e.g. **The ball was kicked. The window was smashed.**

Progress Check

Complete the explanation sentences in 1–3 by adding a connective and a reason.

1 Jane decided not to go out last night . . . .

2 The number of people using public transport has fallen . . .

3 Simon achieved less than 50% in the test . . .

4 What is different about this explanation sentence? *As a result of prolonged rainfall, the river burst its banks.*

(Answers to 1–3 are only possibilities.) **1** because she had too much work to do **2** due to rising fares **3** so he had to re-sit it **4** The connective is at the beginning of the sentence.

7.4 Writing to describe

Describing people

When you describe a person, you might choose to emphasise a particular feature of his or her **appearance** or **personality**. For example: 'My primary school teacher, Mrs Bell, wore brown shoes. She was very kind and rarely shouted.'

To make a piece of writing more interesting, think about other words and phrases you could add to the description to give more information. Try to vary your sentence structure too.

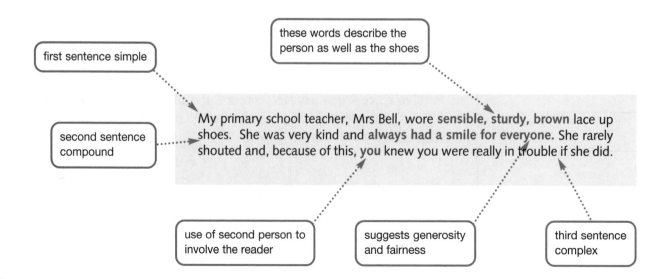

first sentence simple

these words describe the person as well as the shoes

second sentence compound

My primary school teacher, Mrs Bell, wore **sensible, sturdy, brown** lace up shoes. She was very kind and **always had a smile for everyone**. She rarely shouted and, because of this, **you** knew you were really in trouble if she did.

use of second person to involve the reader

suggests generosity and fairness

third sentence complex

If you are asked to describe a person in detail, you need to think about lots of **different aspects** of that person, not just what they look like.

A person I remember clearly from my childhood is my next-door neighbour, Elsie. She was the oldest person I knew. Her skin was like crinkly brown paper and her eyes watered when she laughed. She had delicate, mottled hands and her wedding ring was loose on her finger.

She was generous and kind. Whenever we visited we had jelly sweets or Jaffa cakes. She called me 'wench' or 'ducks'. She always seemed to be washing sheets and took great pride in always being the first out to hang washing on the line.

Describing places

The description that follows is from a piece of fiction. The techniques used in narrative writing can also be used in descriptive non-fiction.

Look out for:

● **imagery** – personification, simile etc.
● **original and adventurous vocabulary**
● **amusing detail**
● **varied sentence structure**
● **sensory description**.

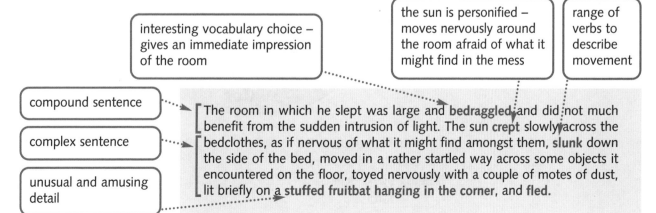

interesting vocabulary choice – gives an immediate impression of the room

the sun is personified – moves nervously around the room afraid of what it might find in the mess

range of verbs to describe movement

compound sentence

complex sentence

unusual and amusing detail

The room in which he slept was large and **bedraggled** and did not much benefit from the sudden intrusion of light. The sun **crept** slowly across the bedclothes, as if nervous of what it might find amongst them, **slunk** down the side of the bed, moved in a rather startled way across some objects it encountered on the floor, toyed nervously with a couple of motes of dust, lit briefly on a **stuffed fruitbat hanging in the corner**, and **fled**.

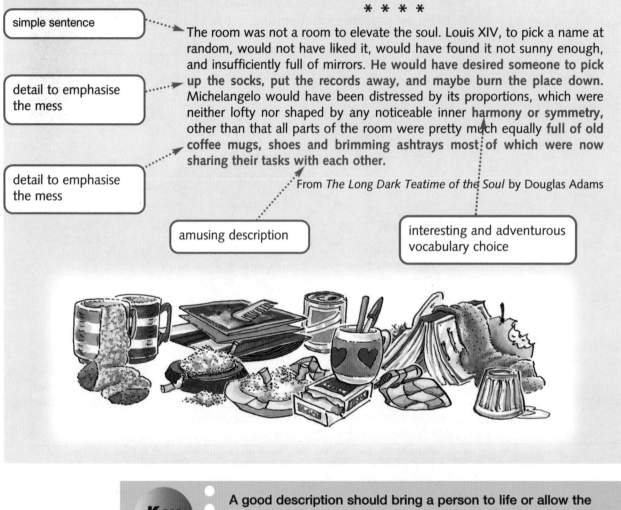

simple sentence

detail to emphasise the mess

detail to emphasise the mess

* * * *

The room was not a room to elevate the soul. Louis XIV, to pick a name at random, would not have liked it, would have found it not sunny enough, and insufficiently full of mirrors. He would have desired someone to pick **up the socks, put the records away, and maybe burn the place down.** Michelangelo would have been distressed by its proportions, which were neither lofty nor shaped by any noticeable inner harmony or symmetry, other than that all parts of the room were pretty much equally **full of old coffee mugs, shoes and brimming ashtrays most of which were now sharing their tasks with each other.**

From *The Long Dark Teatime of the Soul* by Douglas Adams

amusing description

interesting and adventurous vocabulary choice

Key Point

A good description should bring a person to life or allow the readers to visualise themselves in the place or situation described.

Describing memories

You should be able to:
● describe an object, person or setting in a way that includes relevant details and is accurate and evocative.

When you write about a memory, you may have to describe people, places and objects. The plan below is a **brainstorm** for writing about a journey.

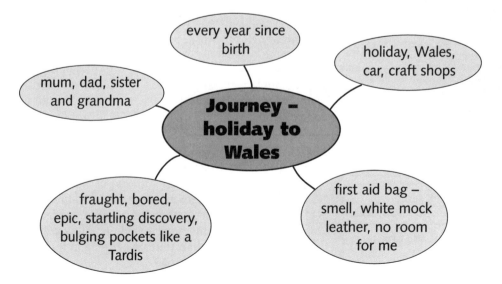

every year since birth

holiday, Wales, car, craft shops

mum, dad, sister and grandma

Journey – holiday to Wales

fraught, bored, epic, startling discovery, bulging pockets like a Tardis

first aid bag – smell, white mock leather, no room for me

Now look at how this planning has been used to start a piece of writing.

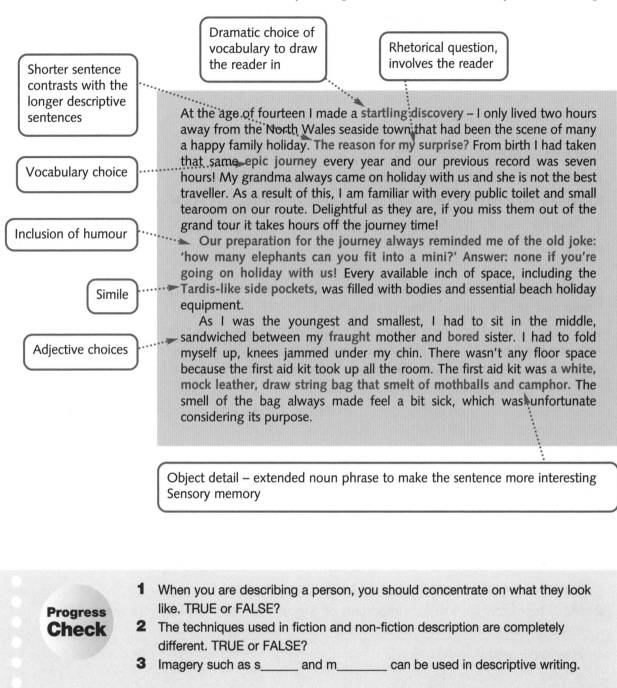

Dramatic choice of vocabulary to draw the reader in

Rhetorical question, involves the reader

Shorter sentence contrasts with the longer descriptive sentences

Vocabulary choice

Inclusion of humour

Simile

Adjective choices

At the age of fourteen I made a **startling discovery** – I only lived two hours away from the North Wales seaside town that had been the scene of many a happy family holiday. **The reason for my surprise?** From birth I had taken that same **epic journey** every year and our previous record was seven hours! My grandma always came on holiday with us and she is not the best traveller. As a result of this, I am familiar with every public toilet and small tearoom on our route. Delightful as they are, if you miss them out of the grand tour it takes hours off the journey time!

Our preparation for the journey always reminded me of the old joke: 'how many elephants can you fit into a mini?' Answer: none if you're going on holiday with us! Every available inch of space, including the **Tardis-like side pockets**, was filled with bodies and essential beach holiday equipment.

As I was the youngest and smallest, I had to sit in the middle, sandwiched between my **fraught** mother and **bored** sister. I had to fold myself up, knees jammed under my chin. There wasn't any floor space because the first aid kit took up all the room. The first aid kit was **a white, mock leather, draw string bag** that smelt of mothballs and camphor. The smell of the bag always made feel a bit sick, which was unfortunate considering its purpose.

Object detail – extended noun phrase to make the sentence more interesting
Sensory memory

1 When you are describing a person, you should concentrate on what they look like. TRUE or FALSE?

2 The techniques used in fiction and non-fiction description are completely different. TRUE or FALSE?

3 Imagery such as s_____ and m_____ can be used in descriptive writing.

1 false   2 false   3 similes and metaphors

Have a go

Write a description of your bedroom, experimenting with some of the techniques discussed above.

Practice test questions

The following questions will help you to prepare for the Optional Tests in Years 7 and 8. Timings and marks are for one question. In the Optional Test there will be a choice of questions. You will be instructed to choose and answer one question, but during your preparation, try to answer all of these questions.

Time: 20 minutes

Assessment: AT3

1 Write a set of **instructions** to get from your house to your school.

2 Write an **information text** about teenage fashions. Write **three** or **four** paragraphs.

3 **Describe** your ideal holiday location. Write **three** or **four** paragraphs.

Marks: 20

The following questions will help you to prepare for SATs in Year 9. The **Writing Paper** will be 1 hour and 15 minutes **including** planning time.

You will be required to complete **two** tasks which test your skills in two of the writing triplets. **Task one is 45 minutes** long and tests: sentence structure and punctuation, text structure and organisation, composition and effect. **Task two is 30 minutes** long and tests: sentence and text organisation, composition and effect, spelling.

These questions test your ability to write to **inform**, **explain and describe**, you should spend 30 minutes answering each question. **Remember**, in the exam you will only complete **one** 30 minute task.

1 **Describe** a place you have enjoyed visiting.

You could write about:

- when and why you visited the place
- why you liked it
- what the place is like
- why you would recommend other people to go there.

2 Many teenagers have to face important or difficult decisions. **Explain** your reasons for making a difficult decision.

You could write about:

- what the decision was
- your options
- your reasons for making the decision
- the effects of your decision.

3 Write an **information** leaflet for teenagers on the dangers of smoking or drinking.

You could write about:

- the physical effects
- reasons why young people drink or smoke
- how to stop or control smoking or drinking.

> Remember, you can invent some of the details you include in an exam.

8 Writing to persuade and argue

After studying this section you should be able to:
- write persuasive letters
- write persuasive speeches
- present persuasive arguments
- present discursive arguments

To achieve the following National Curriculum levels you need to

Level 4
- organise your ideas clearly
- interest and convince your reader

Level 5
- use a formal style where appropriate
- use a range of evidence to support your ideas
- choose vocabulary to create particular effects

Level 6
- develop and sustain your argument
- use sentence structure and punctuation to clarify meaning and create effects

Level 7
- write in a clear and fluent style to persuade or advise, showing an appreciation of audience and purpose
- anticipate and respond to a range of counter-arguments

There are many forms of persuasive writing; some are more obviously persuasive than others. In Chapter 4 Reading non-fiction you will find examples of media persuasive texts: Leaflets (4.3) and Advertisements (4.4). These texts are often designed to persuade the reader to buy something, and therefore the persuasive devices are quite easily identified.

In this chapter a more formal style of persuasion is explored. Letters, speeches and formal arguments are often written to persuade the reader to change their opinion about something. You will learn how to employ persuasive devices in your own writing and to manipulate your sentence structure to make your message or argument more powerful.

 **Key Point** Most persuasive texts use some or all of the following devices: emotive language, repetition, rhetorical questions, presenting opinion as fact.

8.1 Persuasive letters

Letters are often intended to be persuasive. Some examples of persuasive letters are:
- charity or campaign letters
- letters to newspapers expressing an opinion
- a letter of application for a job.

Writing a formal letter

There are lots of **conventions** to follow when writing a formal letter.

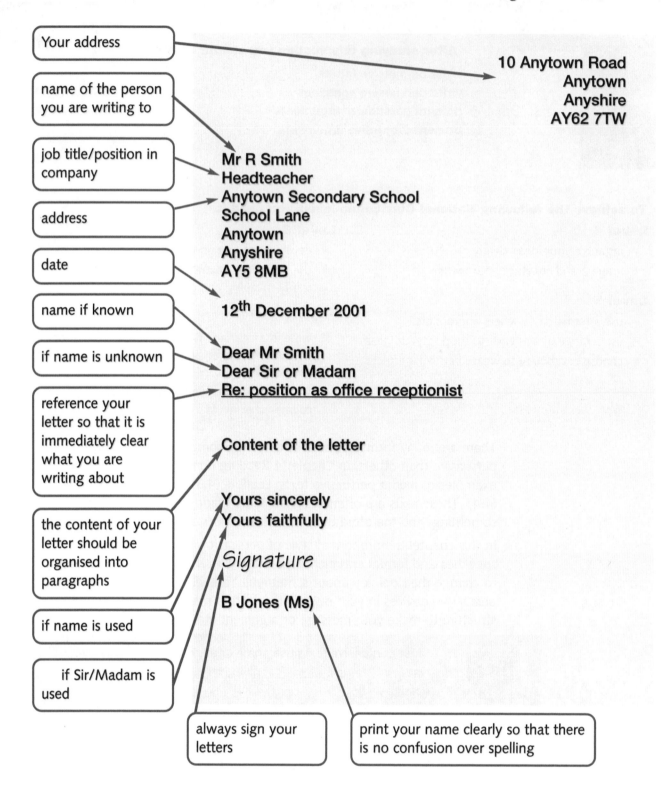

Your address

name of the person you are writing to

job title/position in company

address

date

name if known

if name is unknown

reference your letter so that it is immediately clear what you are writing about

the content of your letter should be organised into paragraphs

if name is used

if Sir/Madam is used

always sign your letters

print your name clearly so that there is no confusion over spelling

10 Anytown Road
Anytown
Anyshire
AY62 7TW

Mr R Smith
Headteacher
Anytown Secondary School
School Lane
Anytown
Anyshire
AY5 8MB

12th December 2001

Dear Mr Smith
Dear Sir or Madam
Re: position as office receptionist

Content of the letter

Yours sincerely
Yours faithfully

Signature

B Jones (Ms)

Key Point

The persuasive devices used in letters are: rhetorical questions and emotive language. Fact and opinion, sentence structure and some visual devices can also be used persuasively.

FRIENDS *of the*
earth
for the planet **for people**

26–28 Underwood Street
London
N1 7JQ

Telephone: 0171 490 1555
Facsimile: 0171 490 0881
Email: info@foe.co.uk
Website: www.foe.co.uk

Dear Mrs Jones

TODAY'S CHOICES CAN SHAPE OUR FUTURE

Our planet faces **terrible dangers**[1]. Greenhouse gases have polluted the atmosphere, causing **dangerous**[1] climate change. Traffic fumes **choke**[1] our cities. One in seven children now suffer from asthma.[2] Every day, vast tracts of rainforest disappear. Meanwhile at home, Government and biotech companies are **trying to force**[1] GM foods on us before they're proved safe.

As an individual, it's easy to **feel helpless**[1] in the face of such huge issues. But we <u>do</u> have a choice.

By supporting Friends of the Earth and starting a regular gift today, you can help bring about a better future.[4]

Friends of the Earth may be a familiar name, but you probably don't know exactly what we achieve, or why. In fact, *The Guardian* has called us *'the UK's most effective environment group'*.[3]

Over the page, you'll find some examples of our successes - major victories for people and the environment won locally, nationally and around the world.

We do this by <u>influencing governments</u> at the highest level. We help communities <u>act locally</u> to protect their environment. And we carry out <u>campaigns and vital research</u> around the world.

Our work is exceptionally effective, but it's only possible with help from people like you.[4] That's why you can make a real difference by turning to the enclosed donation form and supporting Friends of the Earth with a gift of £3 a month. You'll find we've enclosed a pen made from recycled paper to help you fill in the donation form as quickly as possible. If you do not want to keep the pen, please return it to us in the FREEPOST envelope.

If you care about our environment and the world we pass on to our children, please do decide to support us today. You'll be choosing a healthier planet - and a better quality of life for us all. Thank you.[5]

Yours sincerely,

Charles Secrett

Charles Secrett
Executive Director

P.S. If you do not want to keep the pen, please return it to us in the FREEPOST envelope so we can re-use it.

Persuasive devices used in the letter

1 There are many examples of **emotive language** in this letter. Words and phrases have been chosen to make the planet and its inhabitants seem to be in danger. There is also an attempt to make the public seem like the innocent victims of a cruel government: *trying to force....*

2 The writer of this letter has used **facts** persuasively: **One in seven children now suffer from asthma.** The word *now* suggests that things are getting worse as a result of pollution.

3 The writer **quotes other sources** to emphasise the effectiveness of the campaign.

4 **Personal pronouns** are used effectively to make the reader feel that they have the power to make a difference. On the second occasion that this technique is used, it is more persuasive because it is implied that the campaign will fail without the reader's support: *but it's only possible with help from people like you.*

5 The final paragraph is effective because it gives the reader the responsibility for solving the problems that have been described. The first sentence begins with the word *if*. This signals the beginning of a clever, logical argument: **if you care about x then you will do y; therefore, if you don't do y then you don't care about x.** In this case the reader is asked to give money if they care about the environment and their children.

Word level

Using the endings -ous, -ious and -eous.

● **-ous** is the most common ending used to form adjectives: danger ➜ dangerous.

● Use **-ious** if you can hear **shus** at the end of the word, following the letters **t**, **c** or **x**: ambitious, vicious, anxious, or if you can hear **i** as a syllable: obvious.

● Use **-eous** if the root ends in **-ge**: courage ➜ courageous, or if you can hear **e** as a syllable: hideous.

Key Point

A rhetorical question **doesn't require an answer.**

Using rhetorical questions as a persuasive device

A **rhetorical question** does not require or expect an answer. It is used to achieve a stronger emphasis than a direct statement. The speaker or writer assumes that the answer to the question is obvious.

The question, 'How old are you?' clearly requires an answer, whereas the question, 'It makes you think, doesn't it?' assumes that the answer must be yes and doesn't require a response.

This question could be used effectively in a persuasive letter if it followed information intended to make the reader feel uncomfortable. For example:

Many of these homeless people are children as young as 12; children who are forced to live on the streets because of abusive or neglectful family relationships. While we enjoy the comforts of home on a cold winter's night, they are enduring the cold, scrounging for food or change, feeling hungry, cold, dirty and useless. **Makes you think, doesn't it?**

Read the following extract from another charity campaign letter and think about the use of **rhetorical questions**.

> No matter what anyone says, you don't *have* to swallow genetically engineered foods. **Why should you?** It's impossible to quantify the risks they pose – to us or the environment. Once released, it is impossible to control their spread. So, like many people, we at Greenpeace believe they should be banned. **If you feel the same way, why don't you join us?**
>
> You see, the food of the future does not need to be genetically engineered. But if we don't act now, it certainly will be. For example, there's just no way we can contain the spread of genetically engineered pollen once it is free. **I mean, how can you tell the wind which way it should blow pollen, or a bee which flowers it should visit and which it should leave alone?** It will only be a matter of time before natural crops are contaminated with genetically engineered pollen. And then we may never be able to choose what we eat again.

Progress Check

1 If you begin a letter *Dear Sir*, you should end with *Yours sincerely*. TRUE or FALSE?

2 A rhetorical question does not require an answer. TRUE or FALSE?

3 Which of the following questions is mostly likely to be used rhetorically? a) What is your name? b) Why should we pay for the mistakes of others?

1 false 2 true 3 b)

Have a go

Write two paragraphs of a **persuasive** letter about animal cruelty. Try to include emotive language, personal pronouns and at least one rhetorical question.

8.2 Persuasive speeches

Speeches are very important in our society and can be a very powerful way of **persuading** our listeners to change their views. As you read in Chapter 1, the way you deliver a speech is very important. However, in order to deliver a powerful and persuasive speech you have to write it that way first.

The speech printed on page 114 is an extract from one of the most powerful and influential speeches of the twentieth century. It is the final part of a speech delivered by the Reverend Martin Luther King at a civil rights march in Washington DC in the USA on 28th August 1963.

As you read the speech, look at the words and phrases highlighted in different colours and think about why they might be important.

I have a dream . . .

So I say to you, my friends, that even though we must face the difficulties of today and tomorrow, I still have a dream. It is a dream deeply rooted in the American dream that one day this nation will rise up and live out the true meaning of its creed – we hold these truths to be self-evident, that all men are created equal.

I have a dream that one day. on the red hills of Georgia, sons of former slaves and sons of former slave-owners will be able to sit down together at the table of brotherhood.

I have a dream that one day, even the state of Mississippi, a state sweltering with the heat of injustice, sweltering with the heat of oppression, will be transformed into an oasis of freedom and justice.

I have a dream that my four little children will one day live in a nation where they will not be judged by the colour of their skin but by the content of their character. I have a dream today!

I have a dream that one day, down in Alabama, with its vicious racists, with its governor having his lips dripping with the words of interposition and nullification, that one day, right there in Alabama, little black boys and black girls will be able to join hands with little white boys and white girls as sisters and brothers. I have a dream today!

I have a dream that one day every valley shall be exalted, every hill and mountain shall be made low, the rough places shall be made plain, and the crooked places shall be made straight and the glory of the Lord will be revealed and all flesh shall see it together.

This is our hope. This is the faith that I go back to the South with.

With this faith we will be able to bear out of the mountain of despair a stone of hope. With this faith we will be able to transform the jangling discord of our nation into a beautiful symphony of brotherhood.

With this faith we will be able to work together, to pray together, to struggle together, to go to jail together, to stand up for freedom together; knowing that we will be free one day. This will be the day when all of God's children will be able to sing with new meaning — 'my country 'tis of thee; sweet land of liberty, land where my fathers died, land of the pilgrim's pride; from every mountain side, let freedom ring' — and if America is to be a great nation, this must become true.

So let freedom ring from the prodigious hilltops of New Hampshire.

Let freedom ring from the mighty mountains of New York.

Let freedom ring from the heightening Alleghenies of Pennsylvania.

Let freedom ring from the snow-capped Rockies of Colorado.

Let freedom ring from the curvaceous slopes of California.

But not only that.

Let freedom ring from Stone Mountain of Georgia.

Let freedom ring from Lookout Mountain of Tennessee.

Let freedom ring from every hill and molehill of Mississippi, from every mountain side, let freedom ring.

When we let freedom ring, when we let it ring from every village and every hamlet, from every state and every city, we will be able to speed up that day when all of God's children, black men and white men, Jews and Gentiles, Protestants and Catholics, will be able to join hands and sing in the words of the old Negro spiritual, Free at last! free at last! thank God Almighty, we are free at last!'

The main **devices** used in this persuasive speech are:

- repetition
- short exclamatory sentences
- emotive language.

Repetition

All of the highlighted words and phrases in this speech are examples of repetition. Each repeated phrase is used to create a particular effect.

Personal pronouns
- Repeated use of the word *I* indicates a strong personal belief in and attachment to the subject.
- Repeated use of *we* and *our* indicates that this is a shared vision and the speaker wants the audience to be a part of it.

Dream
- Repetition of *I have a dream* shows that this is an ideal vision for the future.
- It shows that the circumstances of the time mean that it can only be a dream. However, the phrase *I have a dream today!* indicates the belief that one day it will be reality.

Freedom
- The words *freedom* and *liberty* are repeated because they are the central theme of his speech.
- Martin Luther King believed that all people should have freedom of speech, freedom of movement, freedom of education and freedom of lifestyle.

Future
- Repetition of phrases such as *one day* emphasise the belief that things will change in the future.
- It also shows that King was prepared to fight for something that he wouldn't necessarily benefit from in his lifetime.

Faith
- The power of this speech comes from the passionate belief that one day the dream will become reality.
- Martin Luther King's **belief** and **faith** are central to the success of this speech.

Key Point

Repetition helps to: reinforce the main points of your speech, build up a rhythm and remind your audience of the main points.

You should be able to:
- express a personal view, adding persuasive emphasis to key points, e. g. *by* reiteration, exaggeration, repetition, *use of* rhetorical questions.

Using repetition in your writing

If you are asked to write a speech about a topic you have strong feelings on, you should begin by **brainstorming**. Think about the important themes, key words, emotions and beliefs that you associate with that topic. These ideas will be the elements that you repeat in your speech.

Although **repetition** is the main device used in this speech, there are other devices that make it a powerful piece of writing.

Emotive language

Martin Luther King's speech has a very honest quality; there is no attempt to manipulate the reader or listener. This is because **emotive language** is used sparingly and selectively.

- *Vicious racists* – at the time that this speech was written, African-Americans were treated as second-class citizens and often suffered violent abuse. The speech could be filled with language like this. The restrained use of language makes occasional references like this more powerful.
- *Beautiful symphony of brotherhood* – use of poetic language to describe freedom emphasises the fact that King sees equality and freedom as beautiful qualities.

> **Key Point**
>
> **Emotive language is the use of words and phrases that evoke an emotional response.**

Using emotive language in your writing

Think of some key **emotive** words or phrases you could use in your speech. Again, you could **brainstorm** your ideas and then select the most powerful and effective words to use in your final speech.

Think carefully about how you could best support the argument you are building. The following words could all be used to describe somebody's death: **died, killed, executed, slaughtered**. Each of these words indicates something different about the person and the circumstances of their death.

- **Died** – this is a neutral word.
- **Killed** – this suggests that somebody else is responsible for the death, but it is still quite a neutral word.
- **Executed** – this suggests that the person who is dead has been killed as a punishment for doing something wrong. This is quite an emotive word as it implies the person deserved to die according to certain value systems.
- **Slaughtered** – this is a very emotive word for two reasons. Firstly, it suggests a very violent and nasty death. Secondly, it implies that we

should make a very different judgment about the person who is dead – they would probably be described as an innocent victim.

If you were writing a speech about the rights or wrongs of **capital punishment**, which of these words would you use?

Sentence structure

Look at the sentence structure of Martin Luther King's speech.

- The first part of the speech is mostly made up of **complex sentences**, which build up pace, **rhythm and momentum**.
- Paragraphs four and five end with a **short exclamatory sentence**. This is in contrast with the rest of the sentences in each paragraph. It is an effective ending to the paragraph, emphasising the power of his vision: *I have a dream today!*
- Towards the end of the speech, the **pace and emphasis changes**. This is reflected in the change of structure.
- Each paragraph is one sentence long and the structure of almost every sentence is exactly the same: *Let freedom ring from the. . . .* This slows the speech down and allows every individual point to be given its own emphasis.

This device is known as a chiasmus.

- The penultimate sentence forms a **reflection** of itself, beginning and ending with the phrase *let freedom ring*.
- The final paragraph **returns** to the earlier pace, with a complex sentence containing all the important ideas visited in the speech. The change in pace allows the **climax** of the speech to be celebratory and defiant.

Using sentence structure in your own writing

Think carefully about the **effects** you are trying to create. Try to use a variety of sentence structures and punctuation to change the pace and emphasis of your speech.

Word level

- Use the ending **-ssion** if there is a **short vowel (a, e or u)** before the **shun** sound: oppression.

- Use the ending **-sion** if you can hear a **zhun** sound: persuasion. **Exceptions**: apprehension, comprehension, mansion, tension.

Progress Check

1 Put these words in order from most emotive to least emotive: *crowd, mob, gang*.

2 Think of a more emotive word to replace the highlighted word in the following headline: 'Train seats **cut** by teenage gang'.

3 Which of the following statements are true? Repetition is a useful device because a) it helps the reader or listener remember the important parts b) you don't need to think of as many points to make c) it builds up a rhythm.

1 mob, gang, crowd **2** slashed **3** a) and c)

8.3 Persuasive argument

Argument is a form of **persuasion**. If you have an argument with somebody, it is because you disagree about something. To win an argument, you must persuade your opponent that your point of view is correct.

A piece of persuasive argument writing is usually quite **formal**. Read the following example and think about the techniques that have been used to persuade the reader that the writer's point of view is correct.

Too much television can damage your child's health

Television may be part of everyday life for most children, but is it safe? In our hectic lives we are so busy managing our private and professional concerns and relationships, we allow our children to spend a huge percentage of their unsupervised time watching television. So busy, in fact, that most of us don't stop to consider the hidden dangers of unlimited viewing.

The health risks which attend excessive television viewing are extensive and, to my mind, should not be underestimated. It contributes to the growing problems of adolescent obesity; it prevents regular exercise, which could cause heart problems in later life; it causes psychological problems if children are exposed to inappropriate materials and it can damage eyesight.

However, the most worrying problem is the detrimental effect that too much television can have on the early stages of a child's development. Playing games, listening to stories and interacting with other children are all essential to a child's emotional, physical and communication development. When television takes the place of these activities, we allow untold damage to be done.

Of course, many would be quick to defend the educational value of television and there is no doubt that properly managed television viewing can be beneficial. In my opinion, however, the dangers far outweigh the benefits. Until parents make time to exercise proper control over their children's viewing habits, children's health will continue to suffer.

How does the text work?

Title

- The title is an opinion presented as a fact. This type of sentence is a **statement**; this gives the writer's opinion authority.

- The statement is shocking and it captures the reader's attention and interest immediately.
- The topic of this piece of argument is immediately obvious.

Structure

The argument is organised into four paragraphs:

1 an introduction setting up the main point of the argument and offering a challenging point of view

2 a range of reasons is given to support the writer's point of view

3 the most important supporting reason is given a paragraph of its own for emphasis

4 the final paragraph concludes the arguement by anticipating a possible counter-argument.

Connectives

The writer uses a range of logical connectives to keep the text varied and interesting:

- *to my mind*
- *however*
- *of course*
- *in my opinion*
- *but*.

Repetition

The second paragraph uses repetition effectively. Each reason why television is damaging is introduced in the same way: *it prevents regular exercise*; *it causes . . . .*

Sentence structure

This is a **formal** piece of writing aimed at an **adult audience**. Most sentences are complex and employ a range of punctuation.

> ### Sentence level
> The language choices we make at **word**, **sentence** and **text level** vary according to audience, purpose, topic and context. Most people make a range of quite sophisticated choices about language, to change the formality of their writing or speech, without even thinking about it.

You should be able to:
- present a case persuasively, making selective use of evidence, using appropriate rhetorical devices and anticipating responses and objections.

Key Point Persuasive argument uses the same devices that have been discussed in topics 8.1 and 8.2.

Writing your own persuasive argument

Plan

First you will need to plan the main points of your argument. The table below shows the points for and against school uniform. Each point '**against**' could be the main point of a paragraph in your argument. You could use the '**for**' points to anticipate and answer any counter-arguments.

School Uniform	
FOR	**AGAINST**
Sense of school identity	Uncomfortable
Smart	Expensive
Easy to identify on trips and visits	Unfashionable
Saves other clothes from wear and tear and subject-related damage, e.g. art, science	Impractical for some subjects
	Prevents expression of personality
	Creates petty discipline problems

Before you begin, you should decide on the best **order** for these points. Think about how you can **link** the different strands of your argument together. You can make some notes below.

_____

_____

_____

_____

_____

A persuasive introduction

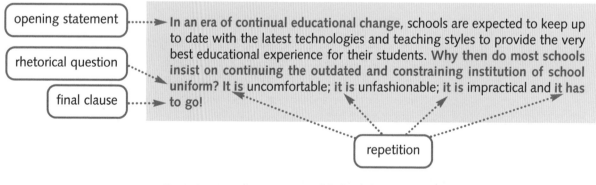

- **Opening statement** – establishes the idea of change.
- **Rhetorical question** – used for emphasis to show that in this area there has been little change.
- **Repetition** – also used for emphasis; each clause in the sentence has the same structure.
- **Final clause** – the change from *it is* to *it has to* adds further emphasis to the final point

Linking the points in your argument

Use a range of connectives, such as:
- **furthermore**
- **another reason for this**
- **not only**
- **on the other hand**
- **despite the fact that**
- **however**
- **nevertheless**.

The following sentence is an **effective link** because it looks back to the previous paragraph of the argument and sets up the next main point:

> Not only is school uniform unfashionable and embarrassing, it is also extremely uncomfortable and impractical.

Anticipating opposition and counter-argument

Try to use **opposing** views to strengthen your own case. If you express **counter-arguments**, you can make them appear weaker than your own. For example:

> Many people contend that school uniform helps to create a sense of school identity and helps students feel that they belong. What other institutions require their members to wear a uniform? Prison is the first example that springs to mind! In prison, inmates lose the freedom to express themselves. School uniform imprisons the wearer, taking away the freedom to express personality and individuality. If schools want to create a sense of identity: why not let students create that identity themselves?

Using evidence to support your argument

If you have **facts or data** to back up your argument, think carefully about how you use them. For example:
- **51%** is better expressed as **over 50%**
- **1 in 8** sounds more impressive than **12%**.

Sentence structure

In **formal** argument you will need to use longer complex sentences in order to express a range of complex ideas. However, controlled use of short, simple sentences for emphasis will make your writing more powerful.

Word level

The example introduction on page 120 uses several prefixes: *uncomfortable*, *unfashionable*, and *impractical*.

A **prefix** is a group of letters added to the beginning of a **root word** to change its meaning. In most cases, adding a prefix does not change the spelling of the root word, even if this means **doubling a consonant** at the beginning of the root word: necessary → unnecessary; satisfied → dissatisfied.

8.4 Discursive argument

Discursive writing is sometimes called a balanced argument because it looks at both sides of the argument, giving each equal weight.

Writing in this style includes:
- **magazine or newspaper articles** that consider all angles of an argument
- **formal essays** that compare and contrast or discuss advantages and disadvantages.

A discursive text

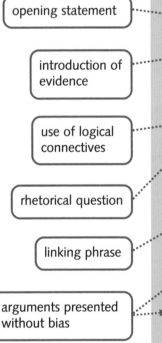

opening statement

introduction of evidence

use of logical connectives

rhetorical question

linking phrase

arguments presented without bias

Many schools in the United Kingdom are beginning to explore the benefits of a more flexible day. Research has shown that children study more effectively during the morning and therefore, some schools are opening their doors earlier to teach more lessons before lunch, leaving the afternoons free for sport and extra-curricular activities. However, many parents oppose the new continental-style day as it interferes with childcare arrangements and means that some children could be left roaming the streets after school has finished.

So what are the benefits? Head teacher, Alan Brown, claims that since changing the structure of the school day, students in all years have achieved greater exam success and there has been a significant reduction in low-level disruption to lessons. His claims are supported by a 5% increase in A*–C grade GCSE passes since the changes were introduced.

However, despite the apparent success of the continental day at Mr Brown's school, critics have warned that it is too early to attribute exam success to the new school day. Many parents believe that the increased workload during the morning session means that students are being expected to work for too long without a proper break. Some students who live 30 minutes away from the school have to wait from 7.30 a.m. until 1.30 p.m. before they have the chance to eat anything. Opponents of the changes claim that lack of rest and nourishment will have a negative effect on examination results in the next few years.

The conventions of a discursive text

- **Opening statement** – this introduces the topic to be discussed.
- *Research has shown* – **connective phrases** are used to introduce evidence.
- **Logical connectives** – phrases such as **therefore, however, despite this, as a result** are used regularly.
- **Rhetorical questions** – are used to introduce argument and counter-argument rather than for persuasive emphasis.
- **Linking phrases** – are used to link paragraphs of argument and counter-argument.
- **Arguments presented without bias** – discursive writing presents the opinions of others, but gives both sides equal weighting. The writer does not give his or her opinion in the main body of the text. The views

expressed in the text are credited to specific people or groups of people, distancing them from the writer or 'narrator'. The writer may sometimes express an opinion favouring the argument or counter-argument in the conclusion.

- **Voice and tense** – discursive writing uses the **present tense** and the **third person**. The **first person** is sometimes used in the conclusion.

- **Structure** – each paragraph or section explores a main point of the argument, followed by the opposing point from the counter-argument.

Using Standard English – formality

This kind of writing requires a **formal style** and you must avoid non-standard forms, as they are inappropriate in argument writing. The following non-standard forms should be avoided.

- Using **adjectives** as **adverbs**:
  She won **easy**. ✗
  She won **easily**. ✔

- Mixing **singular** and **plural** in subject/verb agreement:
  He **were** frightened. ✗
  He **was** frightened. ✔
  We **was** bad. ✗
  We **were** bad. ✔

- Using '**them**' as a **determiner**:
  I bought **them** oranges. ✗
  I bought **those** oranges. ✔

- Using '**what**' as a **relative pronoun**:
  Have you seen the book **what** I bought? ✗
  Have you seen the book **that** I bought? ✔

> The highlighted terms are explained in Chapter 11.

Progress Check

1 A discursive argument looks at all sides of an issue. TRUE or FALSE?
2 When can you give your own opinion in a discursive essay: introduction/main text/conclusion?
3 Change the highlighted non-standard forms in the following sentence: 'We **was** hoping to give you a **real** good present this year.'

1 true   2 conclusion   3 were, really

Have a go
Write a paragraph of argument and counter-argument for the following points about the 'continental school day':

- **Argument** – students can take part in more sport, drama and extra-curricular activities.

- **Counter-argument** – schools can't force students to stay for these activities, so they could be roaming the streets from 2 p.m.

Practice test questions

The following questions will help you prepare for the Optional Tests in Years 7 and 8. In the Optional Test there will be a choice of questions. You will be instructed to choose and answer one question. Timings and marks given below are for one question, but during your preparation, try to answer all of these questions.

Time: 20 minutes

Assessment: AT3

1 Write two or three paragraphs to **persuade** the reader of the need for better leisure facilities in your area.

2 Write four paragraphs of **discursive writing** discussing the advantages and disadvantages of teenagers having mobile phones.

Marks: 20

The following questions will help you to prepare for SATs in Year 9. The **Writing Paper** will be 1 hour and 15 minutes long **including** planning time.

You will be required to complete **two** tasks which test your skills in two of the writing triplets. **Task one is 45 minutes** long and tests: sentence structure and punctuation, text structure and organisation, composition and effect. **Task two is 30 minutes** long and tests: sentence and text organisation, composition and effect, spelling.

These questions test your ability to write to **persuade and argue**, you should spend 45 minutes answering each question. **Remember**, in the exam you will only complete **one** 45 minute task.

1 Imagine you are the director of a new museum.

Write a letter to head teachers of schools in the area **persuading** them to bring groups of pupils to the museum.

You could write about:

● what the museum has to offer

● why it is of educational value

● how to organise a trip there.

2 Imagine you have been given a chance to give a talk to your class. Choose an issue you feel strongly about.

Write a talk trying to **persuade** other people to support your views.

3 Write a **discursive essay** about keeping animals in zoos and safari parks.

Write about:

● points **for** keeping animals in captivity

● points **against** keeping animals in captivity

● your own opinion.

9 Writing to review, analyse and comment

After studying this section you should be able to:

● write a review
● provide analysis and comment on a piece of writing

To achieve the following National Curriculum levels you need to

Level 4
● organise your writing in an informative and interesting way
● comment on the plot and characters in fiction and main stylistic features of non-fiction

Level 5
● use a formal style where appropriate
● select relevant textual evidence to support your comments

Level 6
● comment on the significance and effect of layers of meaning in a text
● justify your views by referring to language, structure and themes

Level 7
● give a personal and critical response to a range of literary texts
● use an appropriately formal style while still engaging the interest of the reader

---

9.1 Writing reviews

When you write a **review** of something you are giving your **own opinion**. This could be completely different from somebody else's opinion on the same topic. You might be asked to write a review about:
● a **book**
● a **film**
● a **television programme**
● an **exhibition**
● a **play**.

What to include

Although a review is made up largely of your **opinion**, you will probably need to provide the reader with some **facts and information**, such as:
● the **title and author/director**, etc.
● a **summary** of the story
● **information** about the exhibition
● **where** you can buy the book or see the film/exhibition/play.

> You should be able to:
> * write reflectively about a text, taking account of the needs of others who might read it.

The **audience** of a written review will usually be people who want to know if they would enjoy the book, film, play or exhibition. You should include your opinions on:
* its **strengths**
* its **weaknesses**
* its **suitability** for a particular audience.

A review of *Kit's Wilderness*

The following extract includes information about the novel *Kit's Wilderness* and discusses its strengths. Notice how the information about the storyline **indicates the writer's opinion** of the book. If he or she thought the story was boring it would have been described in a very different way.

> Whitbread-winning author, David Almond's book *Kit's Wilderness* is about the place where magic and dreams collide with everyday life. Having moved back to the village of Stoneygate, Kit Watson finds himself drawn into John Askew's magical and frightening world. He meets Askew in the wilderness where he must confront life and death.
>
> Almond's writing is elegant and powerful. He manages to speak volumes with the things he doesn't say, while entrancing his readers with what he does. *Kit's Wilderness* is filled with suspense, mystery and wonder. His characters are real, his situations believable and his conclusions satisfying. In fact, *Kit's Wilderness* satisfies on every level.

9.2 Analysis and comment

The **reading** chapters of this study guide (**Chapters 2 to 4**) demonstrate an **analytical style** of writing. Whenever you are asked to write about something you have read, you will be required to comment on or analyse the language, structure or themes of the text. This style of writing is usually very **formal**.

Writing style

The **conventions** of analytical writing are:
* it's written in the **third person**
* **opinions are expressed in a detached way** – avoid phrases such as 'I think that. . .'
* opinions are **supported by textual evidence**
* non-standard forms and colloquial expression should be avoided.

Key Point

Analysis and comment writing is usually a response to a specific question, e.g. Comment on the use of imagery in Wilfred Owen's poem 'Dulce et Decorum Est'.

Structure

An **analytical essay** should follow a set pattern.

- **Introduction** – this should refer to key words in the question, capture the attention of the reader and demonstrate an understanding of the question.
- **Series of paragraphs** – these will explore different aspects of the question. Paragraphs should be linked and main points should be supported with quotation.
- **Conclusion** – this should refer back to the main points of your analysis and give your personal response to the question.

Paragraph structure

A useful way to structure your analysis in each paragraph is:

- make a **statement** or **comment**
- use **quotation** or **textual evidence** to back up your statement
- **explain** your comment with **reference** to the evidence you have cited.

Below is an analysis of Macbeth's soliloquy discussed in **Chapter 2**.

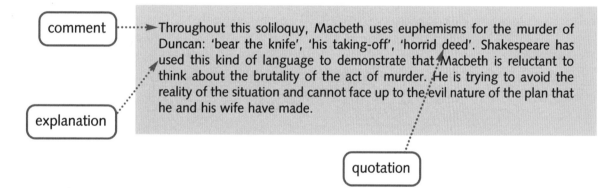

comment

explanation

Throughout this soliloquy, Macbeth uses euphemisms for the murder of Duncan: 'bear the knife', 'his taking-off', 'horrid deed'. Shakespeare has used this kind of language to demonstrate that Macbeth is reluctant to think about the brutality of the act of murder. He is trying to avoid the reality of the situation and cannot face up to the evil nature of the plan that he and his wife have made.

quotation

> You should be able to:
> - cite specific and relevant textual evidence to justify your critical judgements.

Presenting textual evidence

The following examples show how quotations should be set out in your writing.

- **Single words** and **short phrases** should be used as part of the sentence you are writing. The words you are quoting should be placed inside **quotation marks** (inverted commas or speech marks). The rules of punctuation are similar to speech punctuation.

> The poem is ordered by reference to time. In the first stanza all the times are general: **'All year'**, **'every spring'**. The first stanza describes a general interest in nature. It also shows that the collecting of frogspawn is something he does every year and that he is very familiar with the area he describes, having visited it often: **'Daily it sweltered'**.

- Longer quotations of whole sentences or lines of poetry should be presented on a line of their own. Lines of quotation should be slightly **indented** and do not need quotation marks.

> Owen uses two similes to show how tired and ill the soldiers are:
>> Bent double, like old beggars under sacks,
>> Knock-kneed, coughing like hags, we cursed through sludge,
>
> These images are very direct and unpleasant and immediately show that Owen does not believe the sentiment expressed in the title of his poem. During the war, people wanted to imagine brave, healthy soldiers fighting for their country. Owen shows that, although they may have joined the army in that state, the war has damaged them beyond repair.

Progress Check

1 A book review should contain the opinions of the reviewer. TRUE or FALSE?

2 Short phrase quotations should be presented on a line of their own. TRUE or FALSE?

3 Quotations that are presented on a line of their own do not need quotation marks. TRUE or FALSE?

1 true   2 false   3 true

Practice test questions

The following questions will help you to prepare for the Optional Tests in Years 7 and 8. In the Optional Test there will be a choice of questions. You will be instructed to choose and answer one question. Timings and marks given below are for one question, but during your preparation, try to answer all of these questions.

Time: 25 minutes

Assessment: AT3

1 Write a review of the last fiction book you read. You should refer to the strengths and weaknesses of the book.

2 Write a review of a film or television drama you have watched recently, giving your recommendations about who should watch it.

Marks: 20

The following questions will help you to prepare for SATs in Year 9. The **Writing Paper** will be 1 hour and 15 minutes long **including** planning time.

You will be required to complete **two** tasks which test your skills in two of the writing triplets. **Task one is 45 minutes** long and tests: sentence structure and punctuation, text structure and organisation, composition and effect. **Task two is 30 minutes** long and tests: sentence and text organisation, composition and effect, spelling.

These questions test your ability to write to **review**, **analyse and comment**, you should spend 45 minutes answering each question. **Remember**, in the exam you will only complete **one** 45 minute task.

1 Watch two television advertisements for similar products. Write an analysis of the effectiveness of the techniques used to persuade the target audience.

Think about:

- the audience and purpose
- use of music and/or special effects
- use of different camera angles.

2 Write a relationship study on two main characters in a novel you have read recently.

Comment on:

- how the characters are presented to the reader
- how the relationship changes
- how effectively the author conveys this relationship.

The literary criticism questions in Chapter 2 also require you to analyse and comment.

10 Spelling

After studying this section you should be able to:

- use spelling strategies effectively
- understand spelling rules
- understand and use prefixes and suffixes
- use and spell homophones correctly

To achieve the following National Curriculum levels you need to

Level 4

- spell **basic words** and **polysyllabic words** (words with more than one syllable) that fit into regular patterns correctly

Level 5

- spell words with **complex regular** patterns correctly

Level 6

- ensure that spelling, including **irregular** words, is usually accurate

Level 7

- ensure that spelling is always correct, including **complex irregular** words

---

10.1 Spelling strategies

The best ways to improve your spelling are to:
- learn spelling rules
- learn commonly misspelt words
- practise spelling strategies.

Look – Say – Cover – Write – Check

- **Look** at the word you want to learn: try to find patterns; learn the shape of the word.

- **Say** the word.

- **Cover** the word with your hand and **write** it down.

- **Check** your spelling. If you made a mistake, go back to the beginning and look carefully at the part of the word you got wrong.

Use a dictionary

You should be able to:
- make effective use of a **spellchecker**, recognising where it might not be sufficient or appropriate
- use a **dictionary** and a **thesaurus** with speed and skill.

Use a **dictionary** to check the spelling of words you are unsure of. Many dictionaries will also give you **information** about the **roots** and **origins** of words; this is sometimes helpful in learning a new spelling.

You could also use an **electronic spellchecker** or the spellchecker facility on your computer. If you use your computer, make sure it has a UK English checker. Remember that some of the words you use may not be recognised by the computer, particularly names, but this does not mean the spelling is incorrect.

You can't use a dictionary or electronic spellchecker in any kind of English exam, so **make sure you use all of the other strategies for learning spellings too.**

Mnemonics

You should be able to:
- identify words which pose a challenge and learn them by using **mnemonics** and memorising critical features.

Some people find spellings easier to remember if they make up a rhyme to go with them, for example:

Rhythm has your two hands moving.

Big elephants can't always use small exits.

Say the word as it is spelt

You should be able to:
- sound out words phonemically (each sound in a word) and by syllables.

Words that have **silent letters** or **unstressed syllables** in them are often easier to remember if you sound the part of the word that is usually silent. For example:
- Wednesday
- listen
- people.

Break words into parts

Polysyllabic words can be broken into smaller chunks to make them easier to remember. It is almost impossible to spell a word completely incorrectly. Work out which part of a word you find difficult and learn it, for example:

Ex – plan – a – tion

Make a spelling journal

Making a spelling journal will help you to learn spellings you find difficult.
● **Make a record** of all the words you find difficult to spell.
● Get a **list of key words** for each of your school subjects.
● Record some of the **spelling rules** you find helpful and refer to them when you are trying to spell a word you are unsure of.
● **Investigate spelling patterns** and have a go at difficult spellings before asking for help.

10.2 Spelling rules

Plurals

The following rules will help you with your spelling. However, you need to look out for the **exceptions** to these rules. Unfortunately, there are quite a lot of them!

There are some examples for you to try with each rule.

Adding -s and -es

RULE: To make a word into a plural add -s

school ➝ schools   shoe ➝ shoes book ➝ books

If a word ends in -ss, -sh, -ch, -x, -zz add -es

lunch ➝ lunches   glass ➝ glasses   box ➝ boxes

HINT! Words that end in a **hissing**, **shushing** or **buzzing** sound add -es. When you say -es plurals aloud you can hear an extra syllable.

Exceptions

You should be familiar
with spelling rules for:

● pluralisation,
including -es
endings and words
ending in y, f and
vowels.

The other rules and conventions below show the exceptions to the simple
plural rule.

Words that end in -y

RULE: If a word ends in a vowel followed by **-y**, you add **-s**. If a word
ends in a consonant followed by **-y**, you change the **-y** to **-i** and add **-es**.

toy ➜ toy**s**   key ➜ key**s**   try ➜ tr**ies**   factory ➜ factor**ies**

Progress Check

1 Add -s or -es to make the following words plural:
bench, fox, church, pupil, light, wish, wash

2 Add -s or change the ending to make the following words plural:
boy, fly, monkey, play, baby, lady, bay

2 boys, flies, monkeys, plays, babies, ladies, bays
1 benches, foxes, churches, pupils, lights, wishes, washes

Key Point

The rules for words ending in -f and -y apply when you are
adding any other ending.

Words that end in -f, -ff and -fe

Any words that end in **-ff** need an **-s** to make them plural, for example:

sheriff ➜ sheriff**s**   cuff ➜ cuff**s**

Words that end in **-f** or **-fe** are more difficult. Some are made plural by
adding **-s**, such as:

chief ➜ chief**s**   reef ➜ reef**s**

Other words change the **-f** to **-v** and add **-es**, such as:

wife ➜ wi**ves**   leaf ➜ lea**ves**   calf ➜ cal**ves**

Some words that end in **-f** can be spelt with either an **-fs** or a **-ves** plural
ending, such as:

scarf ➜ scarf**s** or scar**ves**   hoof ➜ hoof**s** or hoo**ves**

HINT! As there is no clear rule, **a tip that often works is saying the plural
aloud.** If you can hear a v sound then it usually means the correct spelling
is **-ves**.

cliff**s** = **f** sound   cal**ves** = **v** sound

Irregular plurals

Some plural forms don't seem to follow any of these rules and the whole
word changes, such as:

mouse ➜ **mice**   child ➜ **children**

You need to learn these words as you meet them.

Words that end in -o

Words that end in **-o** or **-oo** don't follow set patterns. Try to group words together as you learn them.

tomato	potato	mango – all edible and all end in **-es**
tomatoes	potatoes	mangoes
tomatoes	potatoes	mosquitoes – they all have **toes** in them

No change plurals

Some words don't change at all! You need to learn these:

sheep   deer   fish

> **Key Point**
>
> Foreign words follow different rules. Learn them as you need them, e.g. cactus → cacti, fungus → fungi.

Progress Check

1 Add **-s** or change the ending to make the following words plural:
wolf, knife, life, loaf, roof

2 What are the plural forms of the following?
man, woman, goose, foot

3 What are the plural forms of the following? Use a dictionary if you need to.
radio, volcano, shampoo, go

3 radios, volcanoes, shampoos, goes
2 men, women, geese, feet
1 wolves, knives, lives, loaves, roofs

10.3 Prefixes and suffixes

Prefixes

You should be familiar with spelling rules for:

- word endings, including vowel suffixes such as *-ing*; consonant suffixes such as *-ful*;
- prefixes.

A **prefix** is a group of two or three letters added to the beginning of a word to change or qualify the meaning, e.g. **dis-, mis-, pre-, un-**.

Rule

When you add a prefix you **do not** change the spelling of the original word:

satisfied → **dis**satisfied
spelling → **mis**spelling
necessary → **un**necessary

> **Key Point**
>
> Remember, prefixes **never** change the root word.

Suffixes

A **suffix** is a group of two or three letters added to the end of a word to make a derivative of the original, e.g. -ed, -ful, -ing, -ly, -ment. Sometimes adding a suffix changes the spelling of the original word.

Rules

Adding a vowel suffix -ed, -ing and -y

If the word has one syllable, one short vowel and ends in a single consonant, you **double the consonant** when you add the ending:

stop ➙ stopped ➙ stopping

fit ➙ fitted ➙ fitting

mud ➙ muddy

Words with more than one syllable or vowel and words that end with a double consonant, take the suffix **without changing the root**:

boss ➙ bossy

deliver ➙ delivery

focus ➙ focusing

groom ➙ groomed

If the word ends in -e you only add the -d of -ed. You omit the -e if you are adding -ing or able:

continue – continued

make – making

excite – excitable

Adding a consonant suffix

In most cases, the root word does not change when you add a suffix that begins with a consonant. Remember the following points.

Adding -ful

RULE: Remember, full becomes -ful. You do not change the original word unless it ends in y (see y ending rule).

fit ➙ fitful

hope ➙ hopeful

Adding -ly

RULE: The original word does not change when you add -ly.

real ➙ really

proper ➙ properly

careful ➙ carefully

Words that end in -le don't follow the same rule. For these words, miss out the final -e and add -y.

responsible ➙ responsibly

possible ➙ possibly

Words ending in -y or -f

The rules for adding suffixes to words ending in **-y** or **-f** are the same as the pluralising rules.

fry → fr**ied**

beauty → beaut**iful**

happy → happ**ily**

play → play**ed**

shelf → shel**ving**

Progress Check

How many words can you make from these prefixes and suffixes?

Prefix	Root	Suffix
mis	appoint	ment
pre	fortunate	ful
dis	view	ly
un	event	ed
	understand	ing

misunderstand, misunderstanding, understanding, understandingly, preview, previewed, previewing, viewed, viewing, viewed, disappoint, disappointment, disappointed, disappointing, disappointingly, appointment, appointed, appointing, uneventful, uneventfully, eventful, eventful, eventually, unfortunate, unfortunately, fortunately

Key Point

Learning prefix and suffix rules will help you to spell polysyllabic words.

10.4 Homophones and commonly misspelt words

Homophones

You should be familiar with:

● the spellings of high-frequency words including common homophones.

There are many words in the English language that sound the same but are spelt differently and have different meanings. They are known as **homophones**.

Many of these are basic words that are commonly used in everyday writing. Look at the table opposite for details of some of the most common homophones. You must learn the spellings of these words.

ARE	present form of the verb to be: Where *are* you going? We *are* all the same age.
OUR	belonging to us: We're going to *our* house.
HEAR	to perceive sound: Can you *hear* me?
HERE	referring to place: Come over *here*.
THEIR	belonging to them: We're going to *their* house.
THERE	referring to place: It's over *there*. indicating the fact or existence of something: *There* is a horse in the field.
THEY'RE	short form of they are: *They're* coming to our house.
THREW	past tense of throw: He *threw* the ball.
THROUGH	He went *through* the door. I read the letter *through*, from beginning to end.

noun

TO	introduces a noun or a verb: Are you going *to* school? I was going *to* walk today.
TOO	also/as well: Can we come *too*? excessive: It was *too* hot. That is *too* expensive.
TWO	the number 2: I ate *two* pieces of cake.

verb

SAW	past tense of see: I *saw* you taking it. tool and action to cut wood: Pass me the *saw*. I will *saw* the plank in half.
SOAR	to fly or rise high: Eagles can *soar* high in the sky.
SORE	painful: My leg was *sore*.
WEAR	of clothes, etc.: I *wear* school uniform.
WERE	past tense of are: We *are* going to school./We *were* going to school.
WE'RE	short form of we are: *We're* going to school.
WHERE	referring to place: *Where* is it?
WHO'S	short form of who is: *Who's* going to be captain?
WHOSE	belonging to: *Whose* bag is this?

Strategies for learning homophones

The best way to ensure that you use homophones correctly is to learn
them. Some ideas that might help you to learn them are:

- look for patterns
- **make groups of words** that have similar spellings or meanings
- draw pictures or cartoons
- make up rhymes.

Key Point

- The word 'there' has many different uses. 'Their' and 'they're' have only one use each. Learn the use of their and they're first; there is used on all other occasions.
- <u>Here</u>, t<u>here</u> and w<u>here</u> are all place words.

Commonly misspelt words

The following words are often spelt incorrectly. It is a good idea to learn
them as they sometimes fail to fit into normal spelling patterns. The parts
of the words that cause confusion or difficulty have been highlighted.

accept**able**	use **able** if the rest of the word will stand alone – **accept**	ne**c**essary	**n**ever **e**at **c**ake **e**at **s**alad **s**andwiches **a**nd **r**emain **y**oung
a**cc**o**mm**odation			**o**ne **c**ollar and two **s**ocks
achi**e**ve	**i before e except after c**	per**m**anent	
analy**s**e		per**s**uade	
a**ss**ess		**ph**ysical	
		rec**ei**ve	**i before e except after c**
beli**e**ve	**i before e except after c**	re**c**o**mm**end	
co**mm**unicate		responsi**ble**	
conven**ie**nt	**i before e except after c**	sepa**r**ate	there's a **rat** in sepa**r**ate
defin**ite**		stationa**ry**	not moving
desp**e**rate		statione**ry**	paper, etc.
		su**cc**e**ss**	
disappear	root words never change when you add a prefix	su**r**prise	
		w**ei**rd	a w**ei**rd exception to the rule!
disappoint	root words never change when you add a prefix		(**i before e except after c**)

Key Point

Don't forget to use LOOK, SAY, COVER, WRITE, CHECK to learn these words.

11 Punctuation and grammar

After studying this section you should be able to:

- use punctuation marks effectively
- use speech punctuation correctly
- use apostrophes correctly
- structure text using paragraphs
- recognise and use sentence types
- recognise and use parts of speech

To achieve the following National Curriculum levels you need to

Level 4
- use **full stops, capital letters** and **question marks** accurately
- begin to use **complex sentences**

Level 5
- use **commas** within a sentence
- use **apostrophes** and **speech marks** correctly
- clearly **structure** your writing **using paragraphs**
- use a **wide range of vocabulary**

Level 6
- use **punctuation** to develop a **range of complex sentences**
- use punctuation to **clarify meaning**

Level 7
- show **increasing control** of a **range of sentence types**
- use punctuation to **clarify meaning** and **create effects**

Key Point

Grammar is the way we organise words to make sense:
- 'This is my dog' is grammatical and it makes sense.
- 'My this is dog' is ungrammatical – it makes no sense at all.

11.1 Punctuation marks

When we talk, we use different tones of voice and pause after certain words to make our meaning clear. When we write, we use **punctuation** to make our meaning clear.

Capital letters and full stops

Capital letters and **full stops** show where a sentence begins and ends:

the cat was sick in the morning we decided to take it to the vet

The cat was sick. In the morning we decided to take it to the vet.

Capital letters are also used for:
- the word **'I'**
- initials – **BBC, RAC**
- names of people, places and products, e.g. **Jane, Brazil, Weetabix.**

Commas

Commas help us to understand the meaning within a sentence. They are used to:

- **separate items in a list**
  You will need a pen, a pencil, a ruler and a rubber.

- **separate additional information (embedded clauses) from the rest of the sentence**

    John, who was very angry, shouted at the children.

- **separate subordinate clauses from main clauses**

    When the rope snapped, the climber fell and broke his leg.

    main

    subordinate

- **after the following words: however, therefore, of course, nevertheless.**

Colons and semicolons

Colons are advanced punctuation marks. They point ahead to something which follows; this could be a quotation in an essay or the beginning of a list.

The **semicolon** is another advanced punctuation mark. It is used to join two sentences that are very closely linked; this may be where a full stop seems too strong and a comma too weak.

Semicolons are also used to separate items in a list when they are phrases rather than single words:

> **Before you go out you should: tidy your bedroom; wash the dishes; feed the cat and hang the washing out.**

11.2 Speech punctuation

Speech marks

Speech marks are essential in your writing to show clearly that someone has spoken. Speech marks are generally used correctly, but there is a lot more to punctuating speech than just speech marks. Here are some basic rules to follow.

Rules

- Speech marks "..." or '...' are placed around the words a person actually speaks.

- The first word inside the speech marks always begins with a **capital letter**.
- The words inside speech marks always end with a **mark of punctuation** (full stop, comma, question mark or exclamation mark).
- If the sentence is continued after the speech marks (with 'he said', etc.), then you don't end the speech with a full stop, and the first word outside the speech marks must begin with a small letter:

  'Tidy your bedroom before you go out,' said my mother.

- If the sentence begins with 'he said', a comma must follow this before you open the speech marks:

  The man turned and whispered, 'Never ask me that again.'

- When a new speaker begins, you must begin a **new paragraph**.

Progress Check

Add the correct punctuation to these sentences.

1 shut up shouted james you don't know what you're talking about
2 i want to go home now mum whispered the bored child
3 i saw james the boy who broke his leg on the bbc news last night
4 when the bell rang the teacher dismissed the class

1 'Shut up!' shouted James, 'You don't know what you're talking about.'
2 'I want to go home now mum,' whispered the bored child.
3 I saw James, the boy who broke his leg, on the BBC news last night.
4 When the bell rang, the teacher dismissed the class.

11.3 Apostrophes

There are two ways to use **apostrophes**:
- to indicate **omission**
- to indicate **possession**.

Apostrophes – omission

Apostrophes are used to show that a letter, or letters, have been missed out when writing a short form. For example: **cannot** becomes **can't**.

If you remember **why** apostrophes are used then you should always get them in the right place.

People often think that the apostrophe goes between the two words that are being joined; this is wrong.

does + not = does'nt ✘

does + not = doesn't ✔

it + is = it's

Apostrophes – possession

Apostrophes are used to show that something belongs to someone or something:

Iqbal's bag – the bag belonging to Iqbal.

- When something belongs to a single person or thing, add apostrophe and s:
  the cat's whiskers; Sally's coat; the boy's homework.
- If the word already ends in s, then just add an apostrophe after the s:
  James' book.
- When something belongs to more than one person or thing, add an apostrophe after the s:
  the cats' whiskers; the girls' bags; ladies' coats.
- If the plural form of a word does not end in s, then add an apostrophe and s:
  the children's homework; the men's hats.
- It is not just objects that belong to people: emotions, people and actions also belong:
  Sunita's anger; Amanda's fear; Leroy's father; the poet's writing.
- 'Belonging to it' does not follow the above rules:
  its = belonging to it
  it's = it is.

Progress Check

1 Write out the short forms of these words using apostrophes:
do not, they will, have not, I am, would not.

2 Add the possessive apostrophes to the phrases below.
the mans strength, the girls bags (singular), the girls bags (plural), yesterdays meeting, Lauras ambition

1 don't, they'll, haven't, I'm, wouldn't
2 man's, girl's, girls', yesterday's, Laura's

11.4 Paragraphs

- A paragraph is a **group of sentences** linked to the same topic.
- Paragraphs help you to **organise** your work.
- In handwriting, indicate paragraphs by **starting a new line and indenting 1 cm from the margin**.

Organising your writing into paragraphs

There are three ways to organise paragraphs:
- by **time**
- by **topic**
- by **talk**.

Look at this extract from *A Kestrel for a Knave*. Notice how the paragraphs are organised.

> ^{TOPIC}Billy tried another rush. Sugden repelled it, so he tried the other end again. Every time he tried to escape the three boys bounced him back, stinging him with their snapping towels as he retreated. . . .
> ^{TIME} When Billy stopped yelling the other boys stopped laughing, and when time passed and no more was heard from him, their conversations began to peter out, and attention gradually focused on the showers. . . .
> ^{TOPIC}The boy guards began to look uneasy, and they looked across to their captain.
> ^{TALK}'Can we let him out now, Sir?'
> ^{TALK}'No!'

11.5 Sentences

There are three types of sentence:
- **simple**
- **compound**
- **complex.**

These sentence types fall into four categories:
- **statements** – The boy laughed. (declarative)
- **questions** – Did you hear me? (interrogative)
- **commands** – Come here now. (imperative)
- **exclamations** – What a mess! (exclamatory)

Simple sentences

A sentence usually contains a **subject** and a **verb**.

subject

phrase (in this case information about where it happens)

My **sister** runs in the park.

verb

Simple sentences give you one main piece of information.

I ran home. I was late. My mum was angry.

Compound sentences

Compound sentences are made up from simple sentences or clauses joined together by conjunctions: **and, but** and **or**. All the clauses have equal weight, as they are all main clauses.

> I ran home. I was late and my mum was angry but she didn't tell me off.

Complex sentences

Complex sentences are made up of two or more clauses, **one of which must be a subordinate clause.** A clause has a **subject** and contains a **verb.**

Subordinate clauses

The subordinate clause in each of the sentences below has been underlined.

Subordinate clauses begin with:

- a **subordinating conjunction** – although, however, because:

  <u>Although her feet hurt</u>, Jane carried on running.

- a **relative pronoun** – **who, which, whose, that.** This kind of subordinate clause is known as a relative clause. You cannot begin a sentence with a relative clause:

  My shoes, <u>which are old and smelly</u>, need to be thrown away.
  I hoped <u>that he would enjoy the match</u>.
  I can see the man <u>whose car was stolen.</u>

> Subordinate clauses give background information, for example: when something happened or how people feel. They help you to create two-part sentences. Subordinate clauses can be used in the first or second half of a sentence; sometimes they can be embedded.

You should be able to:
● recognise and use subordinate clauses; explore the function of subordinate clauses and use subordinate clauses in a variety of positions in a sentence

● a non-finite verb (see **11.6 Parts of speech** for more detail). The non-finite verb form is particularly useful as it allows you to manipulate your sentences and move the subordinate clause around. A non-finite verb can be placed before or after the noun:

<u>Filled with despair</u>, the football manager left the pitch. (**beginning**)
The football manager, <u>filled with despair</u>, left the pitch. (**embedded**)
The football manager left the pitch, <u>filled with despair</u>. (**end**)

Embedded clauses

An **embedded clause** is a subordinate clause that is placed in the middle of a main clause – a bit like a bracketed aside giving extra information.
● The teacher shouted at the children. (**simple sentence**)
● The teacher shouted at the children <u>because he was angry</u>. (**subordinate clause at the end**)
● The teacher, <u>who was filled with anger</u>, shouted at the children. (**embedded subordinate clause**)

Key Point

It is important to use a range of sentences in your writing. This will allow you to create rhythm and interest in your writing.

Progress Check

1 A subordinate clause can stand as a sentence alone. TRUE or FALSE?
2 You can't begin a sentence with a relative clause. TRUE or FALSE?
3 An embedded clause is used at the beginning of a sentence. TRUE or FALSE?

1 false   2 true   3 false

11.6 Parts of speech

Nouns

There are different types of noun:
● **common** – an object you can see or touch, e.g. pen, table, car
● **abstract** – thoughts, ideas, qualities or emotions, e.g. peace, anger, truth
● **collective** – one word indicating a collection of people or objects, e.g. group, herd, queue
● **proper** – an individual name; a place, a person or an object, e.g. Birmingham, Jane, Tower of London.

Noun phrases

A noun phrase is a group of words containing a noun which gives further information about that noun. In the following sentence, the noun phrase is highlighted.

The old, red car parked outside is a nuisance.

A noun phrase can be made up of a number of different elements:
- **head** – this is the noun around which all the other elements are grouped, e.g. **car**
- **determiner** – this comes before the noun and decides what kind of noun is in the phrase: definite, indefinite, common, etc., e.g., **the, some**
- **premodification** – all other words that come before the noun, usually adjectives, e.g. **old, red**
- **postmodification** – all other words in the phrase that come after the noun (head), e.g. **parked outside**.

Pronouns

A **pronoun** takes the place of a **noun** that has already been mentioned: **he, she, it, me, you**. Pronouns can be used as **determiners** Use of pronouns helps to reduce repetition in your writing, e.g.

John picked up **the ball** and threw **the ball** to **John's** friend.
John picked up **the ball** and threw **it** to **his** friend.

Verbs

A verb makes a noun or pronoun work. There are **three** types of verb.
- **Main** – as a general rule you can put the word '**to**' in front of a main verb: **to walk, to dance, to eat**. These are also known as **full verbs**.
- **Auxiliary** – an auxiliary verb helps the main verb: you **should** walk, he **could** dance, I **might** eat.
- **Primary** – **be, have** and **do** can be used as **main** or **auxiliary** verbs:

They **are** happy. (main)
They **are** going. (auxiliary)

Finite and non-finite verbs

The finite form of a verb has to change according to number, person or tense.
- **Tense** – I **work** at home. ➔ I **worked** at home.
- **Number** – She **laughs**. ➔ They **laugh**.
- **Person** – I **am** ➔ You **are**

The non-finite form does not show these contrasts. There are **three** non-finite forms:
- **-ed** participle:
  I **dropped** the pencil.
  He was **dropped** from the team.
  They were **dropped** off on the corner.
- **-ing** participle:
  I'm **running** home tonight.
  They're **running** home tonight.
  He was **running** home last night.
- the **base form** of a verb used as an **infinitive**:
  I'll **see**
  They might **see**
  She wants to **see**.

Adjectives

An **adjective** tells us what a noun is like: **old** book, **sensible** child, **smelly** socks. The use of adjectives in your writing will make it more interesting.

Adverbs

An **adverb** tells us how a verb is done: he walked **quickly**, he danced **stylishly**, I ate **greedily**. This kind of adverb is formed by adding **–ly** to an adjective.

Adverbs can also be the **adverbial** element of a **clause**.

An adverbial can be:

- An adverb phrase containing single adverbs
  He ate the cake **greedily**.
- A **prepositional phrase** – a phrase that begins with a preposition
  He ran **to the bus stop**.
- Some sub-ordinate clauses (adverbial clauses)
  I asked him **when he came into the office**.

Adverbials usually answer the question **where**, **when** or **how**.

Many of the descriptions contained in the grammar section are very **brief and general**. For further detail and explanation you should **use a grammar textbook**.

Practice test answers

Chapter 2

Optional Test

You should include the following points in your answers.

1 *blundered, walked, stumbled, climbed, shuffled, moved*

They add variety and make the characters seem uncertain.

2 It is a long, complex sentence with lots of clauses; it is repetitive; it creates the effect of a desperate search for Skellig, looking everywhere and getting frustrated.

3 The characters whisper; it's very dark; they are uncertain; there is detail about how they respond to their situation *our breath was fast, shallow, trembly*; short sentences are used to build up tension; longer sentences create the sense of a search going on.

SATs Practice

The following general guidance indicates some of the main features you should include in your writing about Shakespeare.

1 Staging question: make links between how characters feel and the way they move and speak; pick out specific lines and speeches that are important and give instructions about how these lines should be delivered and how other characters should respond; show your understanding of the whole play by commenting on differences and similarities; connect your instructions for this part of the play to instructions you would give for other parts of the play.

2–6 Literary criticism questions: write in a formal style, building your argument and explanation point by point; respond to the key words in the question; limit the amount of plot summary you use; use statement – evidence – explanation/comment in each paragraph; comment on the way language is used; link your scene to other parts of the play; comment on character behaviour and motivation; make comments about the way this scene would be staged to create the atmosphere and reveal relationships.

Chapter 3

Optional Test

1 The boy is playing hide and seek; the boy's friends look for him but then give up and run away; the boy waits for a long time on his own.

2 lonely and nervous

3 Short sentences create tension – he's holding his breath, waiting to be found; question mark shows he's alert to every sound, he seems jumpy and wonders with each noise if they will find him; exclamation marks show fear and excitement.

4 They are the voice of the boy; these are the words he calls out in the game and after his friends have gone.

SATs practice

You could comment on the following features of the poem:

● life/blood images, *thickened wine*, *palms sticky as Bluebeard's*, *rat grey fungus*

● sentence structure from *Then red ones inked up...* , link structure to the movement of the children, shorter sentences in the second stanza

● excitement in the first stanza, disappointment in the second stanza

● voice of the child: *it wasn't fair / That all the lovely canfuls...*

● the sound of the words – *milk-cans*, *pea-tins*, *jam-pot*

● contrast between words like *knot* and *blobs*

● loss of childhood innocence.

Give a personal response.

Chapter 4

Optional Test

1 33

2 paragraph 6

3 headline, picture, caption, short paragraphs

4 the first sentence

5 *Epic*: makes the journey sound longer, more exciting and dramatic; *hero*: makes Robert sound unstoppable.

SATs Practice

You could comment on the following features of the leaflet:

Content: balance of information about events and persuasive language; information about new events; emphasis on fun for 'kids'.

Language: use of emotive persuasive language – *splendour, relax, rare, fascinating, precious, Aladin's Cave of treasures, unique* – comment on the effectiveness of these words; use of words linked to discovery and adventure; use of second person to involve the reader; use of the phrase *it's free* on front the cover.

Layout:

- Pictures – front cover: smiling children appeal to the family, steam train appeals to sense of tradition; inside panel: smiling children, families smiling together, lots of 'hands-on' pictures to show that the exhibitions are interactive .

- Font styles – *it's free* stands out from the background; the rest of the writing on the front cover makes it inviting and appealing, it invites the reader to turn over and open the leaflet up; the text inside the leaflet is in a standard font style and size, it easy to read and suits the informative purpose of the text.

- Other features – the text is organised by sub-headings; bullet points are used to make the new exhibitions stand out; the whole leaflet is colourful and attractive.

- Effectiveness – include your personal response to the leaflet; decide whether the features you have commented on are used effectively.

Chapter 6

Optional Test

Include vocabulary to create a frightening atmosphere Use a range of complex, compound and simple sentences. Experiment with withholding information to increase tension. Make sure you have a balance of narrative, description and dialogue. Review your vocabulary choices for describing the way characters speak. Give clues about characters, as well as giving explicit description.

SATs Practice

Make imaginative vocabulary choices to create an atmosphere. Use a range of complex, compound and simple sentences. Experiment with withholding information to increase tension. Experiment with narrative perspective and style. Make sure you have a balance of narrative, description and dialogue. Review your vocabulary choices for describing the way characters speak. Give clues about characters as well as giving explicit description. Develop characterisation and relationships in the middle section of your narrative.

Chapter 7

Optional Test

1 Logical steps or short paragraphs; mostly simple sentences; use imperative; use a range of time connectives; write in the present tense.

2 Introductory paragraph giving an overview of the topic; organise paragraphs by category/topic; use third person; give examples.

3 Use imagery; make imaginative adjective and adverb choices; use a range of complex, compound and simple sentences; describe different aspects of the location – landscape, atmosphere, people, attractions and things to do.

SATs Practice

1 Answer each bullet point; use imagery; make imaginative adjective and adverb choices; use a range of complex, compound and simple sentences; describe different aspects of the location – landscape, atmosphere, people, attractions and things to do.

2 Answer each bullet point; use logical, cause and effect connectives; organise into paragraphs.

3 Include information on each of the bullet points; use a range of layout devices; organise information for maximum impact; write in the third person; you could include more personal examples; include facts and statistics.

Chapter 8

Optional Test

1 Write a persuasive introduction; use emotive and persuasive language; use rhetorical questions and statements; use repetition for emphasis; anticipate possible objections and defend against counter-argument.

2 Write a paragraph that introduces the argument and counter-argument; organise paragraphs by argument and counter-argument; give equal weight to each side of the argument; don't give personal opinions except in the conclusion.

SATs Practice

1 Answer each bullet point; follow conventions for a formal letter; balance information with persuasive language.

2 Use emotive and persuasive language; use rhetorical questions, statements and exclamations; use repetition for emphasis; anticipate possible objections and defend against counter-argument; use sentence structure to control the pace and emphasis of the speech.

3 Write a paragraph that introduces the argument and counter-argument; organise paragraphs by argument and counter-argument; give equal weight to each side of the argument; don't give personal opinions except in the conclusion.

Chapter 9

Optional Test

Include factual information about the piece being reviewed; give your own opinions; consider strengths and weaknesses; justify your opinions with textual evidence, if appropriate; give recommendations.

SATs Practice

Answer each bullet point; organise paragraphs to build on each point made; use statement – evidence – comment/explanation in each paragraph; follow conventions for including textual evidence; use a formal style; analyse use of particular devices, language or structure where appropriate.

Glossary

Literary terms

Imagery

Image a picture painted with words. Imagery is used to bring ideas to life and make unusual connections that cause the reader to think.

Metaphor an assertion that one object is a completely different object – there is no comparison made. *His words were icy splinters lodged in her heart*; (of an onion) *it is a moon wrapped in brown paper* (from *Valentine* by Carol Ann Duffy).

- **Extended metaphor** a metaphor built up from a number of images in a longer piece of text. An extended metaphor can be made up of similes, metaphors and other images.

Oxymoron the joining of two words or phrases that appear to be complete opposites in meaning: *feather of lead, bright smoke, cold fire, sick health* (from Shakespeare's *Romeo & Juliet*).

Personification an inanimate (not moving/living) object is given the qualities or actions of a living person or creature: *brightly coloured beach balls dance along the shore.*

Simile a comparison of two distinctly different objects using the words **like** or **as**: *The peasants came like swarms of flies* (from *Night of the Scorpion* by Nissim Ezekiel).

Key Point Try to use the correct technical terms when you are writing about literature.

Device

Alliteration the repetition of a letter or letter sound at the beginning of a sequence of words. Used for emphasis and to link ideas: *the silver snake slithered silently by.*

Assonance the repetition of identical or similar vowel sounds in a sequence of words: *silent, quiet light, time* (long 'i' sound).

Onomatopoeia the sound of a word reflects the sound that it describes: *plop, fizz, splash, hiss.*

Structure

Caesura   a pause in the middle of a line of poetry or a sentence in prose, used for dramatic effect: *That's where we played Askew's game, the game called death*. (From *Kit's Wilderness* by David Almond.)

End-stopped line   in poetry, a full stop or colon at the end of a line causes the reader to pause. This technique is used in combination with enjambment.

Enjambment   this is the technical term for a 'run on line'. When the meaning of one line runs into the next line, there is no punctuation at the end of the line. This technique is used to create a sense of movement or excitement in a poem.

Free verse   describes a poem that has a free structure, without a regular rhyme scheme, rhythm or stanza length.

Rhyme   the ending of one word sounds the same as another: *late*/*fate*, *sight*/*might*, *health*/*wealth*

- **End rhymes**   the most common form of rhyme. These rhymes occur at the end of a verse line.

- **Internal rhyme**   these occur in the middle of a verse line: *In mist or cloud, on mast or shroud* (from the *Rime of the Ancient Mariner* by S T Coleridge).

Rhyme scheme   the method of describing rhyme patterns in a poem.

Rhythm   the pattern of beats or stresses in a line or group of lines of poetry, also known as the **meter**.

Stanza   the correct technical term for a verse in poetry.

Other terms

Empathy   writers put themselves in the place of the person or object they are writing about; a stronger sensation than sympathy. If you empathise with somebody, you can understand how they feel and feel their sadness, relief or other emotions yourself.

Narrative   a story told in prose or poetic form. See **Chapter 6** for an explanation of narrative voices.

Narrator   the voice that tells the story.

Key Point   Don't just identify images or devices. You must explain why they are effective.

Glossary of media terms

Newspaper

Broadsheet   a newspaper considered to be more factual and serious than a tabloid. Aims to inform, report and comment, not to entertain. Broadsheets are the larger of the two newspaper styles, e.g. *The Guardian*, *The Times*.

Columns   newspapers and magazine articles are set out in columns; leaflets often use this format too. Columns break up a page and make it more interesting to look at.

Headlines   in newspapers, headlines are particularly important attention grabbers. They are made deliberately dramatic so that the audience will read on. In tabloid newspapers, headlines are often linked to pictures to make up the majority of the front page. Language devices such as alliteration, repetition and rhyme are often used.

Pictures   are used in newspapers to back up, dramatise or personalise a story. They are often closely linked to headlines.

Quotation   a direct comment taken from somebody involved in the news story. This gives the report validity and can often give a more personal feel to the story. Reporters are required to be unbiased, but quotations from other sources will often contain bias.

Short paragraphs   long paragraphs can be off-putting for a busy reader. Most media texts are organised into short paragraphs to hold the reader's attention.

Tabloid   this kind of newspaper is considered to be less serious and sometimes less factual than a broadsheet. Tabloids are also more likely to contain obvious bias. As well as reporting, these newspapers also aim to entertain. They are the smaller of the two newspaper styles, e.g. *The Sun*, *The Mirror*.

Topic sentence   the first sentence in a newspaper story; usually closely linked to the headline. It answers the *who*, *what*, *where* and *when* questions.

Advertisements

Personal pronouns   in persuasive writing, particularly advertising and charity campaigns, the pronouns *you* and *we* are used extensively. This is to make the reader feel personally addressed and important.

Pictures   in advertising, the picture can be more important than the text.

Slogans   are like a 'catch phrase' linked to the product. Various devices are used to make them more memorable: alliteration, repetition, puns, questions or shocking statements.

Text size   important information is in large print; less appealing information, such as terms and conditions, tends to be in smaller print.

Leaflets

Bold print   darker print makes important information stand out from the rest of the text.

Bullet points   often marked out with an asterisk or small symbol, these short sentences or phrases attract the attention of a busy reader.

Font styles   different styles of printing are used to a make a text look more attractive.

Frames and borders   sections of text may be presented within a border or box to make them stand out or to separate them from other information.

Graphs and charts are used to demonstrate facts and figures in a clear visual way.

Pictures are often used in an emotive way in leaflets, e.g. a picture of a starving African child or a lonely pensioner.

Sub-headings are used as signposts to indicate important information in any text. Key words and phrases are picked out to focus the reader's attention.

Other terms

Audience a term to describe the readership that a particular text is aimed at. In advertising, a lot of market research is done so that products can be aimed at very specific groups of people – the people most likely to buy the product.

Market research is used by advertising companies to find out the preferences of an identified group of people. The information collected will influence decisions about colours, music, language, age and styling of actors used in advertising campaigns, as well as the pricing and packaging of products.

Tone of voice this indicates the emotions and feelings that the writer wishes to convey. It is easy to identify a tone of voice when somebody is speaking to you; it is more difficult to identify the tone of a piece of writing. You can identify tone of voice by examining the vocabulary choices, formality, structure and content of a piece of writing. Tones of voice you might expect to find in media texts are: persuasive, conversational, informative, tempting, dramatic or conspiratorial. You wouldn't expect the tone to be aggressive or superior, as this would be off-putting.

Useful information and sources

Useful Websites

For more information or help with a particular topic try some of the websites below

For more information about Shakespeare
www.shakespeare-online.com
www.allshakespeare.com
www.shakespeares-globe.org

For more information about William Blake
www.tate.org.uk/britain/exhitions/blakeinteractive
www.newi.ac.uk/rdover/blake

War Poetry
www.spartacus.schoolnet.co.uk

Improve your writing
www.englishonline.co.uk/writers

For help with Spelling, Punctuation and Grammar
www.funbrain.com
www.4learning.co.uk/fairground

General English
www.learn.co.uk
www.englishonline.co.uk

If you have enjoyed reading the extracts in this book, why not try reading more by the same author?

Fiction and Literary Non-Fiction

Douglas Adams	*The Dark Teatime of the Soul*
David Almond	*Kit's Wilderness*
	Skellig
Bill Bryson	*Notes from a Small Island*
Barry Hines	*A Kestrel for A Knave*
Laurie Lee	*Cider With Rosie*
J K Rowling	*Harry Potter and the Philosopher's Stone*
John Steinbeck	*Of Mice and Men*
Robert Swindells	*Room 13*
	Stone Cold
H G Wells	*The Red Room*

Poetry

William Blake	*Songs of Innocence and Experience*
Charles Causley	*Collected Poems*
Pie Corbett	*An Odd Kettle of Fish*
Carol Ann Duffy	*Mean Time*
Nissim Ezekiel	*Latter Day Poems*
Seamus Heaney	*New Selected poems 1966–87*
Rudyard Kipling	*A Choice of Kipling's Verse*
Wilfred Owen & Rupert Brook	*Penguin Book of First World War Poetry*

Acknowledgements

The authors and publisher are grateful to the copyright holders for permission to use quoted materials: p10: Martin Luther King, Jr., *I Have A Dream* reprinted by arrangement with the Estate of Martin Luther King, Jr., c/o Writers House as agent for the proprietor New York, NY. Copyright 1963 Dr. Martin Luther King Jr., copyright renewed 1991 Coretta Scott King; pp17, 18, 19: J K Rowling, *Harry Potter and the Philosopher's Stone* (Bloomsbury Publishing Plc, 1997, reprinted by permission of the author and Christopher Little Literary Agency); p20: David Almond, *Kit's Wilderness* (Hodder and Stoughton Publishers, London, 1999, reprinted by permission of the publisher and David Almond); pp22–23: Barry Hines, *A Kestrel for a Knave* (Michael Joseph, 1968 copyright © Barry Hines, 1968, reprinted by permission of The Penguin Group (UK); pp25–26: Robert Swindells, *Room 13* (Heinemann New Windmill, 1998, reprinted by permission of Transworld Publishers. All rights reserved; p36: David Almond, *Skellig* (Hodder and Stoughton Publishers, London, 1998, reprinted by permission of the publisher and David Almond); p39: Charles Causley, "What has happened to Lulu?" from *Collected Poems* (Picador, London); p40: Rudyard Kipling "A way through the woods" from *A Choice of Kipling's Verse* (ed. T.S. Elliot) (Faber and Faber Ltd, London, 1963); p41: Pie Corbett, "City Jungle" from *An Odd Kettle of Fish* (eds. Pie Corbett, Brian Moses and John Rice) (Macmillan Children's books, London); p42: Nissim Ezekiel, "Night of the Scorpion" from *Latter Day Poems* (Oxford University Press, India, 1998); Carol Ann Duffy, "Valentine" from *Mean Time* (Anvil Poetry Press Ltd, 1993); p44: "Over the wintry" from *Cricket Songs: Japanese Haiku* (trans. Harry Behn 1964); Seamus Heaney "Death of a Naturalist" from *New Selected Poems 1966–1987* (Faber and Faber Ltd, London); p46: William Blake, "Holy Thursday" from *Songs of Innocence*; p47: William Blake, "Holy Thursday" from *Songs of Experience*; p50: Wilfred Owen, "Dulce et Decorum Est" from *The Penguin Book of First World War Poetry* (2 ed) (ed. Jon Silkin) (Penguin Books Ltd., 1981); p51: Rupert Brooke, "The Soldier" from *The Penguin Book of First World War Poetry* (2 ed) (ed. Jon Silkin) (Penguin Books Ltd., 1981); p54: Vernon Scannell, "Hide and Seek" from *Wordscapes* (ed. Barry Maybury) (Oxford University Press, Oxford, 1970); p55: Seamus Heaney "Blackberry Picking" from *New Selected Poems 1966–1987* (Faber and Faber Ltd, London); p57: Laurie Lee, *Cider with Rosie* (Chatto & Windus Ltd, 1970, reprinted by permission of The Random House Group Ltd); pp61, 62–63: © Bill Bryson. Extracted from *Notes From A Small Island* by Bill Bryson, published by Black Swan, a division of Transworld Publishers. All rights reserved; pp63–64: "The Upright Ape", reprinted by permission of The Yorkshire Museum, York; p69: "Black Watch Cruise" advertisement, reprinted by permission of Page & Moy Ltd, Fred Olsen Cruises; p73: "Robert's One Gump Ahead in Long Run" Manchester Evening News 8.8.2000; p74: "National Railway Museum Leaflet" 2001, reprinted by permission of the National Railway Museum, York; p84: Barry Hines, *A Kestrel for a Knave* (Michael Joseph, 1968 copyright © Barry Hines, 1968, reprinted by permission of The Penguin Group (UK); p85: John Steinbeck, *Of Mice and Men* (Mandarin Paperbacks, 1992, reprinted by permission of Curtis Brown Group Ltd.); Iain M Banks *Excession* (Orbit books, 1996, reprinted by permission of Time Warner Books and the author); pp86–87: H G Wells, "The Red Room" from *Stories Then and Now* (Heinemann New Windmill 1997, with permission of A P Watt Ltd on behalf of the Literary Executors of the Estate of H G Wells); pp89, 90–91: David Almond, *Kit's Wilderness* (Hodder and Stoughton Publishers, London, 1999, reprinted by permission of the publisher and David Almond); p93: Robert Swindells, *Stone Cold* (Hamish Hamilton, 1993) Copyright © Robert Swindells, 1993, reprinted by permission of The Penguin Group (UK); p97: Sue Penny, Judaism (Heinemann Educational Books, Oxford, 1987); p99: "Volunteering" leaflet, reprinted by permission of Help The Aged; p101: "Recipe for Buttered Tagliatelle with Parmesan" from *Easy Pasta* (Octopus Publishing Group, London, 1999); pp105–106: Douglas Adams, *The Long Dark Teatime of the Soul* (Pan Books Ltd, 1987); p111: "Today's Choices Can Shape Our Future" reprinted by permission of Friends of the Earth; p113: "GM statement" reprinted by permission of Greenpeace; p114: Martin Luther King, Jr., *I Have A Dream* reprinted by arrangement with the Estate of Martin Luther King, Jr., c/o Writers House as agent for the proprietor New York, NY. Copyright 1963 Dr. Martin Luther King Jr., copyright renewed 1991 Coretta Scott King.

Every effort has been made to trace the copyright holders and to obtain their permission for the use of copyright material. The author and publisher will gladly receive information enabling them to rectify any error or omission in subsequent editions.

Index